To:

....

From:

....

Date:

....

Life
IN HIS
Presence

A Jesus Calling®

GUIDED JOURNAL

Sarah
Young

THOMAS NELSON
Since 1798

Published in Nashville, Tennessee, by Thomas Nelson. Thomas Nelson is a registered trademark of HarperCollins Christian Publishing, Inc.

Unless otherwise noted, Scripture quotations are taken from the Holy Bible, New International Version®, NIV®. Copyright © 1973, 1978, 1984 by Biblica, Inc.® Used by permission of Zondervan. All rights reserved worldwide. www.Zondervan.com. The "NIV" and "New International Version" are trademarks registered in the United States Patent and Trademark Office by Biblica, Inc.®

Scripture quotations marked KJV are from the King James Version. Public domain.

Scripture quotations marked NASB are from New American Standard Bible®. Copyright © 1960, 1962, 1963, 1968, 1971, 1972, 1973, 1975, 1977, 1995 by The Lockman Foundation. Used by permission. (www.Lockman.org)

Scripture quotations marked NKJV are from the New King James Version®. © 1982 by Thomas Nelson. Used by permission. All rights reserved.

Any Internet addresses, phone numbers, or company or product information printed in this book are offered as a resource and are not intended in any way to be or to imply an endorsement by Thomas Nelson, nor does Thomas Nelson vouch for the existence, content, or services of these sites, phone numbers, companies, or products beyond the life of this book.

ISBN 978-1-4002-1927-8

Printed in Canada

20 21 22 23 24 TR 6 5 4 3 2

Introduction

Dear Reader,

May the pages of this book help you grow a deeper relationship with God and learn to experience peace in the presence of our Savior.

I have written from the perspective of Jesus speaking to you, the reader, to help you feel more personally connected with Him. So the first person singular ("I," "Me," "My," "Mine") always refer to Jesus; "you" refers to you, the reader. I've included Scripture references with each devotion, and I encourage you to read both—slowly and prayerfully.

This selection of much-loved devotions from *Jesus Calling®* alongside journaling prompts and space for reflection will help you look forward to your time with the Lord. Experience a deeper relationship with Jesus as you savor the presence of the One who understands you perfectly and loves you forever!

Sarah Young

For He Himself is our Peace.

EPHESIANS 2:14, NKJV

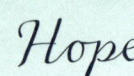

Hope

We have this hope as an anchor for the
soul, firm and secure. It enters the inner
sanctuary behind the curtain.

HEBREWS 6:19

HOPE IS A GOLDEN CORD connecting you to heaven. This cord helps you hold your head up high, even when multiple trials are buffeting you. I never leave your side, and I never let go of your hand. But without the cord of hope, your head may slump and your feet may shuffle as you journey uphill with Me. Hope lifts your perspective from your weary feet to the glorious view you can see from the high road. You are reminded that the road we're traveling together is ultimately a highway to heaven. When you consider this radiant destination, the roughness or smoothness of the road ahead becomes much less significant. I am training you to hold in your heart a dual focus: My continual Presence and the hope of heaven.

Today's reading describes hope as "a golden cord connecting you to heaven." What does this connection mean for us in our daily walk with Jesus?

....

....

....

....

Hope is the thing that "lifts your perspective from your weary feet to the glorious view you can see from the high road." How have you seen the truth of this statement in your life?

....

....

....

....

First Thessalonians 5:8 describes the hope of salvation as a helmet. How does hope—and its promise of salvation—protect our minds and thoughts?

....

....

....

....

READ MORE: ROMANS 12:12; 1 THESSALONIANS 5:8; HEBREWS 6:18–19

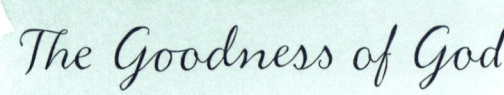

The Goodness of God

For the Lord is good; His mercy is everlasting,
and His truth endures to all generations.

PSALM 100:5 NKJV

Taste and see that I am good. This command contains an invitation to experience My living Presence. It also contains a promise. The more you experience Me, the more convinced you become of My goodness. This knowledge is essential to your faith-walk. When adversities strike, the human instinct is to doubt My goodness. My ways are mysterious, even to those who know Me intimately. *As the heavens are higher than the earth, so are My ways and thoughts higher than your ways and thoughts.* Do not try to fathom My ways. Instead, spend time enjoying Me and experiencing My goodness.

> *The more you experience Me, the more convinced you become of My goodness.*

"Taste and see that I am good" is a command, an invitation, and a promise (Psalm 34:8). How is it each of these three things?

....

....

....

....

The goodness of God is all around. Write about a time you experienced God's goodness.

....

....

....

....

Why is His goodness essential to our faith-walk, especially in times of adversity?

....

....

....

....

Read More: Psalm 34:8; Isaiah 55:8–9

Thankfulness

This is the day the LORD has made;
let us rejoice and be glad in it.

PSALM 118:24

COME TO ME WITH A THANKFUL HEART so that you can enjoy My Presence. This is the day that I have made. I want you to rejoice *today*, refusing to worry about tomorrow. Search for all that I have prepared for you, anticipating abundant blessings and accepting difficulties as they come. I can weave miracles into the most mundane day if you keep your focus on Me.

Come to Me with all your needs, knowing that *My glorious riches* are a more-than-adequate supply. Stay in continual communication with Me so that you can live above your circumstances even while you are in the midst of them. *Present your requests to Me with thanksgiving, and My Peace, which surpasses all comprehension, will guard your heart and mind.*

Read Philippians 4:6–7. How are we to lift up our prayers to God?

....

....

....

....

Even in troubling times, God wants us to choose thankful rejoicing over worry. How does a focus on thankfulness defeat worry and offer opportunities for rejoicing?

....

....

....

....

Write out a prayer asking God to supply your needs and thanking Him for all He has done and will do in your life.

....

....

....

....

READ MORE: PHILIPPIANS 4:19; PHILIPPIANS 4:6–7 NASB

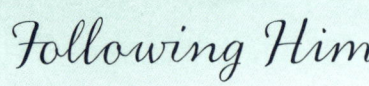

Following Him

"When he has brought out all his own, he
goes on ahead of them, and his sheep follow
him because they know his voice."

JOHN 10:4

I LOVE YOU FOR WHO YOU ARE, not for what you do. Many voices vie for control of your mind, especially when you sit in silence. You must learn to discern what is My voice and what is not. Ask My Spirit to give you this discernment. Many of My children run around in circles, trying to obey the various voices directing their lives. This results in fragmented, frustrating patterns of living. Do not fall into this trap. Walk closely with Me each moment, listening for My directives and enjoying My Companionship. Refuse to let other voices tie you up in knots. *My sheep know My voice and follow Me wherever I lead.*

> *I love you for who you are,
> not for what you do.*

How does listening to God's truths help us respond to the world's opinion of who we should be?

....

....

....

....

John 10:4 says that Jesus' sheep follow Him because they know His voice. How can we be more intentional about listening for the voice of Jesus?

....

....

....

....

What helps tune out others' voices and focus on God? Write a prayer asking God to quiet the voices of the world so you can focus on Him.

....

....

....

....

READ MORE: EPHESIANS 4:1–6

His Presence

"She will give birth to a son, and you are to give
him the name Jesus, because he will save his
people from their sins. . . . The virgin will be with
child and will give birth to a son, and they will call
him Immanuel"—which means, "God with us."

MATTHEW 1:21, 23

I AM *GOD WITH YOU*, for all time and throughout eternity. Don't let the familiarity of that concept numb its impact on your consciousness. My perpetual Presence with you can be a continual source of Joy, springing up and flowing out in streams of abundant Life. Let your mind reverberate with meanings of My Names: Jesus, *the Lord saves*; and Immanuel, *God with us*. Strive to remain conscious of My Presence even in your busiest moments. Talk with Me about whatever delights you, whatever upsets you, whatever is on your mind. These tiny steps of daily discipline, taken one after the other, will keep you close to Me on the path of Life.

How does the never-ceasing Presence of God impact our lives—our worries, thoughts, and actions?

....

....

....

....

What daily disciplines help remind you that God is always with you?

....

....

....

....

Jesus invites you to step into His Presence and tell Him about "whatever delights you, whatever upsets you, whatever is on your mind." What can you tell Him today?

....

....

....

....

READ MORE: JOHN 10:10 NKJV; ACTS 2:28

Rest

"Come to me, all you who are weary and burdened,
and I will give you rest. Take my yoke upon you
and learn from me, for I am gentle and humble
in heart, and you will find rest for your souls."

MATTHEW 11:28–29

COME TO ME AND REST. I am all around you, to bless and restore. Breathe Me in with each breath. The way just ahead of you is very steep. Slow down and cling tightly to My hand. I am teaching you a difficult lesson, learned only by hardship.

Come to Me and rest.

Lift up empty hands of faith to receive My precious Presence. Light, Life, Joy, and Peace flow freely through this gift. When your focus turns away from Me, you grasp for other things. You drop the glowing gift of My Presence as you reach for lifeless ashes. Return to Me; regain My Presence.

How is the rest found in God's Presence different from simply resting our bodies and minds in sleep?

....

....

....

....

How might prayer—especially prayer with "empty hands of faith"—lead to rest?

....

....

....

....

Spend a few moments simply breathing in the Presence of God. Resolve to spend a part of each day resting in Him. Write a commitment here.

....

....

....

....

....

READ MORE: 1 TIMOTHY 2:8; ZECHARIAH 1:3

17

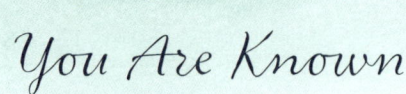

You Are Known

My frame was not hidden from you when I was made in the secret
place. When I was woven together in the depths of the earth,
your eyes saw my unformed body. All the days ordained for me
were written in your book before one of them came to be.

PSALM 139:15–16

I DESIGNED YOU to live in union with Me. This union does not
negate who you are; it actually makes you more fully yourself.
When you try to live independently of Me, you experience emptiness and dissatisfaction. You may *gain the whole world* and yet
lose everything that really counts.

Find fulfillment through living close to Me, yielding to My
purposes for you. Though I may lead you along paths that feel
alien to you, trust that I know what I am doing. If you follow Me
wholeheartedly, you will discover facets of yourself that were
previously hidden. I know you intimately—far better than you
know yourself. In union with Me, you are complete. In closeness to Me, you are transformed more and more into the one I
designed you to be.

God knows us better than we know ourselves. How is this truth a comfort?

....

....

....

....

....

Read Psalm 139:13–16. How might God's intimate knowledge of us and of every day of our lives help us face an unknown and uncertain future?

....

....

....

....

....

How does closeness to God transform us into who He would have us be?

....

....

....

....

....

Read More: Mark 8:36; Psalm 139:13–16; 2 Corinthians 3:17–18

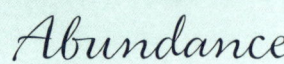

Abundance

When they had all had enough to eat, he said to his disciples,
"Gather the pieces that are left over. Let nothing be wasted." So
they gathered them and filled twelve baskets with the pieces
of the five barley loaves left over by those who had eaten.

JOHN 6:12–13

I AM A GOD of both intricate detail and overflowing abundance. When you entrust the details of your life to Me, you are surprised by how thoroughly I answer your petitions. I take pleasure in hearing your prayers, so feel free to bring Me all your requests. The more you pray, the more answers you can receive. Best of all, your faith is strengthened as you see how precisely I respond to your specific prayers.

> I take pleasure in hearing your prayers.

Because I am infinite in all My ways, you need not fear that I will run out of resources. *Abundance* is at the very heart of who I AM. Come to Me in joyful expectation of receiving all you need—and sometimes much more! I delight in showering blessings on My beloved children. Come to Me with open hands and heart, ready to receive all I have for you.

How have you experienced both the "intricate detail" and "overflowing abundance" of God?

....

....

....

....

....

....

Have you ever been surprised by how thoroughly God answers prayer? What does this reveal about Him?

....

....

....

....

....

....

Read More: Psalm 36:7–9; Psalm 132:15; John 6:12–13

Anxiety and Fear

In addition to all this, take up the shield
of faith, with which you can extinguish all
the flaming arrows of the evil one.

EPHESIANS 6:16

BRING ME ALL YOUR FEELINGS, even the ones you wish you didn't have. Fear and anxiety still plague you. Feelings per se are not sinful, but they can be temptations to sin. Blazing missiles of fear fly at you day and night; these attacks from the evil one come at you relentlessly. Use your *shield of faith to extinguish those flaming arrows.* Affirm your trust in Me, regardless of how you feel. If you persist, your feelings will eventually fall in line with your faith.

Do not hide from your fear or pretend it isn't there. Anxiety that you hide in the recesses of your heart will give birth to fear of fear: a monstrous mutation. Bring your anxieties out into the Light of My Presence, where we can deal with them together. Concentrate on trusting Me, and fearfulness will gradually lose its foothold within you.

How do we hide from our fears or pretend they aren't there?

....

....

....

....

....

What happens to worries, fears, and anxieties when we bring them to Jesus?

....

....

....

....

....

Write out a prayer professing your trust in Jesus and releasing your fearfulness to Him.

....

....

....

....

....

READ MORE: ISAIAH 12:2; 1 JOHN 1:5–7

Every Moment

Pray continually.

1 THESSALONIANS 5:17

YOU NEED ME EVERY MOMENT. Your awareness of your constant need for Me is your greatest strength. Your neediness, properly handled, is a link to My Presence. However, there are pitfalls that you must be on guard against: self-pity, self-preoccupation, giving up. Your inadequacy presents you with a continual choice—deep dependence on Me or despair. The emptiness you feel within will be filled either with problems or with My Presence. Make Me central in your consciousness by *praying continually*: simple, short prayers flowing out of the present moment. Use My Name liberally, to remind you of My Presence. *Keep on asking and you will receive, so that your gladness may be full and complete.*

> *You need Me every moment.*

Do you believe you need Jesus every moment? In what ways does your life reflect this belief?

....

....

....

....

....

How does neediness "properly handled" link us to God's Presence?

....

....

....

....

....

How can you pray continually, even in the busyness of your day?

....

....

....

....

....

READ MORE: PSALM 86:7; JOHN 16:24 AMP

Time with Him

Look to the LORD and his strength;

seek his face always.

PSALM 105:4

RELAX IN MY HEALING PRESENCE. As you spend time with Me, your thoughts tend to jump ahead to today's plans and problems. Bring your mind back to Me for refreshment and renewal. Let the Light of My Presence soak into you as you focus your thoughts on Me. Thus I equip you to face whatever the day brings. This sacrifice of time pleases Me and strengthens you. Do not skimp on our time together. Resist the clamor of tasks waiting to be done. *You have chosen what is better, and it will not be taken away from you.*

> *I equip you to face whatever the day brings.*

How does time in Jesus' Presence heal and bless us?

....

....

....

....

....

What tempts us to "skimp on our time together" with Him?

....

....

....

....

....

How can you better resist the demands of tasks waiting to be completed and relax in His healing Presence?

....

....

....

....

....

READ MORE: PSALM 89:15; LUKE 10:39–42

Follow Me

With your help I can advance against a
troop; with my God I can scale a wall.

PSALM 18:29

FOLLOW ME ONE STEP AT A TIME. That is all I require of you. In
fact, that is the only way to move through this space-time world.
You see huge mountains looming, and you start wondering how
you're going to scale those heights. Meanwhile, because you're
not looking where you're going, you stumble on the easy path
where I am leading you now. As I help you get back on your feet,
you tell Me how worried you are about the cliffs up ahead. But
you don't know what will happen today, much less tomorrow.
Our path may take an abrupt turn, leading you away from those
mountains. There may be an easier way up the mountains than
is visible from this distance. If I do lead you up the cliffs, I will
equip you thoroughly for that strenuous climb. *I will even give
My angels charge over you, to preserve you in all your ways.*

Keep your mind on the present journey, enjoying My Presence.
Walk by faith, not by sight, trusting Me to open up the way before you.

In what ways do you struggle to focus on the present?

....

....

....

....

....

What helps us to follow Jesus "one step at a time" and not worry about the future or regret the past?

....

....

....

....

....

Of all the things we worry about, are any of them insurmountable with God beside us? Why? How does this make you feel?

....

....

....

....

READ MORE: PSALM 91:11–12 AMP; 2 CORINTHIANS 5:7 NKJV

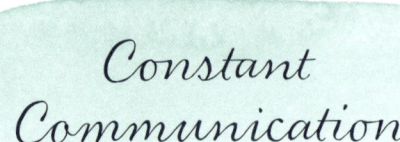

Constant Communication

Since we live by the Spirit, let us
keep in step with the Spirit.

GALATIANS 5:25

I AM CALLING YOU to a life of constant communion with Me. Basic training includes learning to live above your circumstances, even while interacting on that cluttered plane of life. You yearn for a simplified lifestyle so that your communication with Me can be uninterrupted. But I challenge you to relinquish the fantasy of an uncluttered world. Accept each day just as it comes, and find Me in the midst of it all.

Talk with Me about every aspect of your day, including your feelings. Remember that your ultimate goal is not to control or fix everything around you; it is to keep communing with Me. A successful day is one in which you have stayed in touch with Me, even if many things remain undone at the end of the day. Do not let your to-do list (written or mental) become an idol directing your life. Instead, ask My Spirit to guide you moment by moment. He will keep you close to Me.

What might "constant communication" with God look like in your day-to-day life?

....

....

....

....

What changes can you make in order to deepen your communication with God?

....

....

....

....

"I challenge you to relinquish the fantasy of an uncluttered world." Do you daydream about an uncluttered world? Why is it so important to be able to find God amid the clutter?

....

....

....

....

READ MORE: 1 THESSALONIANS 5:17; 3:6

Cease Striving

"Woe to you, teachers of the law and Pharisees,
you hypocrites! You shut the kingdom of heaven
in men's faces. You yourselves do not enter, nor
will you let those enter who are trying to."

MATTHEW 23:13

RELAX IN MY HEALING, holy Presence. *Be still* while I transform your heart and mind. *Let go* of cares and worries so that you can receive My Peace. *Cease striving, and know that I am God.*

Do not be like Pharisees who multiplied regulations, creating their own form of "godliness." They got so wrapped up in their own rules that they lost sight of Me. Even today, man-made rules about how to live the Christian life enslave many people. Their focus is on their performance, rather than on Me.

It is through knowing Me intimately that you become like Me. This requires spending time alone with Me. *Let go, relax, be still, and know that I am God.*

"Cease striving, and know that I am God." Why must we cease striving in order to know that God is God? Are there areas of striving you need to release to Him?

....

....

....

....

Are you striving with a man-made rule? How can you seek out God's rule instead?

....

....

....

....

Take time to "let go, relax, be still, and know that I am God." Use this space to reflect on your experience.

....

....

....

....

READ MORE: PSALM 46:10 NASB; 1 JOHN 3:2

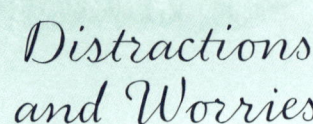

Distractions and Worries

For God is not the author of confusion but of
peace, as in all the churches of the saints.

1 CORINTHIANS 14:33 NKJV

LET THE DEW OF MY PRESENCE refresh your mind and heart. So many, many things vie for your attention in this complex world of instant communication. The world has changed enormously since I first gave the command to *be still, and know that I am God.* However, this timeless truth is essential for the well-being of your soul. As dew refreshes grass and flowers during the stillness of the night, so My Presence revitalizes you as you sit quietly with Me.

A refreshed, revitalized mind is able to sort out what is important and what is not. In its natural condition, your mind easily gets stuck on trivial matters. Like the spinning wheels of a car trapped in mud, the cogs of your brain spin impotently when you focus on a trivial thing. As soon as you start communicating with Me about the matter, your thoughts gain traction and you can move on to more important things. Communicate with Me continually, and I will put My thoughts into your mind.

34

Read Luke 10:39–42. Martha was upset and distracted by many things. What are the things that worry and distract you?

....

....

....

....

God is the author of peace, even "in this complex world of instant communication." How can we invite His peace into our lives?

....

....

....

....

....

Write out a prayer asking God to fill your mind with His thoughts.

....

....

....

....

....

READ MORE: PSALM 46:10; LUKE 10:39–42

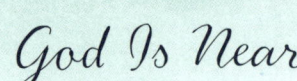

God Is Near

> "Indeed, the very hairs of your head are
> all numbered. Don't be afraid; you are
> worth more than many sparrows."
>
> LUKE 12:7

NEVER TAKE FOR GRANTED My intimate nearness. Marvel at the wonder of My continual Presence with you. Even the most ardent human lover cannot be with you always. Nor can another person know the intimacies of your heart, mind, and spirit. *I know everything about you—even the number of hairs on your head.* You don't need to work at revealing yourself to Me.

I, the Lover of your soul, understand you perfectly and love you eternally.

Many people spend a lifetime or a small fortune searching for someone who understands them. Yet I am freely available to all who call upon My Name, who open their hearts to receive Me as Savior. This simple act of faith is the beginning of a lifelong love story. I, the Lover of your soul, understand you perfectly and love you eternally.

What does God's "ultimate nearness" mean? Do you take His Presence for granted? How?

....

....

....

What comfort does God's loving knowledge—even the number of hairs on your head—provide?

....

....

....

We are not only fully known and understood but also eternally loved. What assurances does this give?

....

....

....

READ MORE: PSALM 145:18 NKJV; JOHN 1:12; ROMANS 10:13

Hide in Him

How great is Your goodness, which You have
stored up for those who fear You, which You have
wrought for those who take refuge in You.

PSALM 31:19

REFRESH YOURSELF in the Peace of My Presence. This Peace
can be your portion at all times and in all circumstances. Learn
to *hide in the secret of My Presence*, even as you carry out your
duties in the world. I am both with you and within you. I go
before you to open up the way, and I also walk alongside you.
There could never be another companion as devoted as I am.

Because I am your constant Companion, there should be
a lightness to your step that is observable to others. Do not be
weighed down with problems and unresolved issues, for I am
your burden-bearer. In the world you have trials and distress,
but don't let them get you down. *I have conquered the world and
deprived it of power to harm you.* In Me you may have confident
Peace.

What does it mean to "hide in the secret of My Presence"?

....

....

....

....

....

How can we hide in Him even as we go about our daily lives?

....

....

....

....

How does Jesus' Presence refresh you with Peace?

....

....

....

....

....

READ MORE: PSALM 31:19–20 NASB; JOHN 16:33 AMP

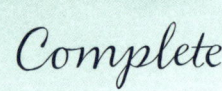

Complete

Now to him who is able to do immeasurably
more than all we ask or imagine, according to his
power that is at work within us, to him be glory
in the church and in Christ Jesus throughout
all generations, for ever and ever! Amen.

EPHESIANS 3:20–21

IN ME YOU HAVE EVERYTHING. In Me you are complete. Your capacity to experience Me is increasing through My removal of debris and clutter from your heart. As your yearning for Me increases, other desires are gradually lessening. Since I am infinite and abundantly accessible to you, desiring Me above all else is the best way to live.

It is impossible for you to have a need that I cannot meet. After all, I created you and everything that is. The world is still at My beck and call, though it often appears otherwise. Do not be fooled by appearances. *Things that are visible are brief and fleeting, while things that are invisible are everlasting.*

"In Me you have everything." What does this mean to you?

....

....

....

....

....

How does being "in" God complete us?

....

....

....

....

....

"It is impossible for you to have a need that I cannot meet." How important is this truth to your faith?

....

....

....

....

....

READ MORE: 2 CORINTHIANS 4:18 AMP

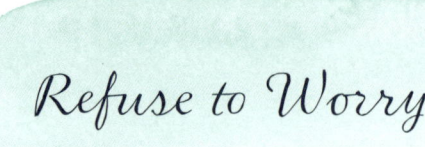

Refuse to Worry

For with you is the fountain of life;
in your light we see light.

PSALM 36:9

REFUSE TO WORRY! In this world there will always be something enticing you to worry. That is the nature of a fallen, fractured planet: Things are not as they should be. So the temptation to be anxious is constantly with you, trying to worm its way into your mind. The best defense is *continual communication with Me, richly seasoned with thanksgiving.* Awareness of My Presence fills your mind with Light and Peace, leaving no room for fear. This awareness lifts you up above your circumstances, enabling you to see problems from My perspective. Live close to Me! Together we can keep the wolves of worry at bay.

When does worry most plague you? How can you defend against it?

....

....

....

....

....

How is "continual communication with [Jesus], richly seasoned with thanks-giving" the best defense against worry?

....

....

....

....

....

Write out your worries here, and prayerfully entrust them to Jesus' care.

....

....

....

....

....

READ MORE: LUKE 12:25–26; 1 THESSALONIANS 5:16–18

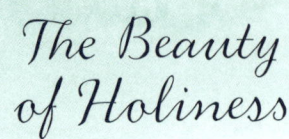

The Beauty of Holiness

Give unto the LORD the glory due to His name;
worship the LORD in the beauty of holiness.

PSALM 29:2 NKJV

MEET ME IN MORNING STILLNESS, while the earth is fresh with the dew of My Presence. *Worship Me in the beauty of holiness.* Sing love songs to My holy Name. As you give yourself to Me, My Spirit swells within you till you are flooded with divine Presence.

> Sing love songs to My holy Name.

The world's way of pursuing riches is grasping and hoarding. You attain *My* riches by letting go and giving. The more you give yourself to Me and My ways, the more I fill you with *inexpressible, heavenly Joy.*

What does it mean to worship the Lord "in the beauty of holiness"?

....

....

....

....

"The world's way of pursuing riches is grasping and hoarding," yet God's riches are found through "letting go and giving." What can you let go of and give—both *to* Him and *for* Him?

....

....

....

....

Make a plan to spend time with God in the morning. Journal about that meeting with Him here.

....

....

....

....

....

Read More: Psalm 9:10; 1 Peter 1:8

Chasing Perfection

Delight yourself in the LORD and he will
give you the desires of your heart.

PSALM 37:4

REMEMBER THAT YOU LIVE IN a fallen world: an abnormal world
tainted by sin. Much frustration and failure result from your
seeking perfection in this life. There is nothing perfect in this
world except Me. That is why closeness to Me satisfies deep
yearnings and fills you with Joy.

I have planted longing for perfection in every human heart.
This is a good desire, which I alone can fulfill. But most people
seek this fulfillment in other people and earthly pleasures or
achievements. Thus they create idols, before which they bow
down. *I will have no other gods before Me!* Make Me the deepest
desire of your heart. Let Me fulfill your yearning for perfection.

"Much frustration and failure result from your seeking perfection in this life." Are you chasing after perfection? How does the desire for perfection impact your faith?

....

....

....

....

God realizes we are not perfect. Do you find comfort in this truth? Why?

....

....

....

....

What might change if you stopped chasing after your own perfection and turned your focus to God's perfection?

....

....

....

....

....

READ MORE: ROMANS 8:22; EXODUS 20:3

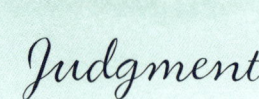

Judgment

He saved us, not because of righteous things we had
done, but because of his mercy. He saved us through
the washing of rebirth and renewal by the Holy Spirit.

TITUS 3:5

MY CHILDREN make a pastime of judging one another—and
themselves. But I am the only capable Judge, and I have acquitted you through My own blood. Your acquittal came at the price of My unparalleled sacrifice. That is why I am highly offended when I hear My children judge one another or indulge in self-hatred.

There is no condemnation for those who belong to Me.

If you live close to Me and absorb My Word, the Holy Spirit
will guide and correct you as needed. There is *no condemnation*
for those who belong to Me.

Do you struggle with judging others? With judging yourself? How?

....

....

....

....

....

Why is God the only capable Judge?

....

....

....

....

....

Read Romans 8:1. For those who choose to follow Him, is there any need to fear God's judgment? How does this make you feel?

....

....

....

....

....

READ MORE: LUKE 6:37; 2 TIMOTHY 4:8; ROMANS 8:1

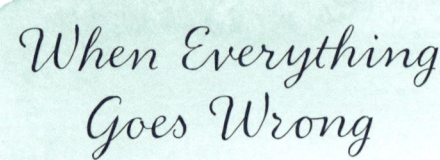

When Everything Goes Wrong

He makes my feet like the feet of a deer; he
enables me to stand on the heights.

PSALM 18:33

WHEN THINGS SEEM to be going all wrong, stop and affirm your trust in Me. Calmly bring these matters to Me, and leave them in My capable hands. Then, simply do the next thing. Stay in touch with Me through thankful, trusting prayers, resting in My sovereign control. Rejoice in Me—exult in the God of your salvation! As you trust in Me, *I make your feet like the feet of a deer. I enable you to walk and make progress upon your high places of trouble, suffering, or responsibility.*

> *Stay in touch with Me through thankful, trusting prayers.*

When everything seems to be going wrong, how do humans usually respond?

....

....

....

....

....

What might happen if we chose to affirm our trust in God during these times?

....

....

....

....

....

Many people like to plan out everything, down to the tiniest details, especially in times of trouble. Yet God asks us to trust Him with our troubles and "simply do the next thing." What is the "next thing" for you?

....

....

....

....

READ MORE: JOB 13:15 NKJV; HABAKKUK 3:17–19 AMP

His Path

To shine on those living in darkness and in the shadow
of death, to guide our feet into the path of peace.

LUKE 1:79

YOU ARE ON THE PATH of My choosing. There is no randomness about your life. Here and Now comprise the coordinates of your daily life. Most people let their moments slip through their fingers, half-lived. They avoid the present by worrying about the future or longing for a better time and place. They forget that they are creatures who are subject to the limitations of time and space. They forget their Creator, who walks with them only in the present.

Every moment is alive with My glorious Presence, to those whose hearts are intimately connected with Mine. As you give yourself more and more to a life of constant communion with Me, you will find that you simply have no time for worry. Thus, you are freed to let My Spirit direct your steps, enabling you to walk along *the path of Peace.*

"There is no randomness about your life." Does this truth change our perspective about all the little and not-so-little moments that fill our days?

....

....

....

....

God walks with us "only in the present." What does this tell us about time spent on future worries and past regrets?

....

....

....

....

Are worries preventing you from living fully right now? How can "constant communion" with God free you from those worries?

....

....

....

....

....

READ MORE: LUKE 12:25–26; JUDE vv. 24–25

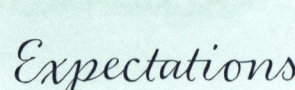

Expectations

The bolts of your gates will be iron and bronze,
and your strength will equal your days.

DEUTERONOMY 33:25

WALK PEACEFULLY WITH ME through this day. You are wondering how you will cope with all that is expected of you. You must traverse this day like any other: one step at a time. Instead of mentally rehearsing how you will do this or that, keep your mind on My Presence and on taking the next step. The more demanding your day, the more help you can expect from Me. This is a training opportunity since I designed you for deep dependence on your Shepherd-King. Challenging times wake you up and amplify your awareness of needing My help.

> *When you don't know what to do, wait while I open the way before you.*

When you don't know what to do, wait while I open the way

before you. Trust that I know what I'm doing, and be ready to follow My lead. *I will give strength to you, and I will bless you with Peace.*

How are expectations—from others, from yourself, from God—weighing on you?

....

....

....

....

How can you keep your mind focused on God's Presence during stressful times?

....

....

....

....

How can you strengthen your trust in and dependence on God?

....

....

....

....

READ MORE: EXODUS 33:14; HEBREWS 13:20–21; PSALM 29:11

Soak in His Presence

Within your temple, O God, we
meditate on your unfailing love.

PSALM 48:9

I AM LIFE AND LIGHT IN ABUNDANCE. As you spend time "soaking" in My Presence, you are energized and lightened. Through communing with Me, you transfer your heavy burdens to My strong shoulders. By gazing at Me, you gain My perspective on your life. This time alone with Me is essential for unscrambling your thoughts and smoothing out the day before you.

Be willing to fight for this precious time with Me.

Be willing to fight for this precious time with Me. Opposition comes in many forms: your own desire to linger in bed; the evil one's determination to distract you from Me; the pressure of family, friends, and your own inner critic to spend your time more productively. As you grow in your desire to please Me above all else, you gain strength to resist these opponents. *Delight yourself in Me, for I am the deepest Desire of your heart.*

When was the last time you "soaked" in the Presence of God?

....

....

....

....

Time with God is essential. Why is it so hard to set aside that time for Him? How could you change that?

....

....

....

....

What form does "opposition" to time with God take in your life? How can you fight it?

....

....

....

....

READ MORE: DEUTERONOMY 33:12; PSALM 37:4

Protected

The LORD appeared to us in the past, saying: "I have loved you
with an everlasting love; I have drawn you with loving-kindness."

JEREMIAH 31:3

I LOVE YOU with an everlasting Love, which flows out from the depths of eternity. Before you were born, I knew you. Ponder the awesome mystery of a Love that encompasses you from before birth to beyond the grave.

Modern man has lost the perspective of eternity. To distract himself from the gaping jaws of death, he engages in ceaseless activity and amusement. The practice of being still in My Presence is almost a lost art, yet it is this very stillness that enables you to experience My eternal Love. You need the certainty of My loving Presence in order to weather the storms of life. During times of severe testing, even the best theology can fail you if it isn't accompanied by experiential knowledge of Me. The ultimate protection against sinking during life's storms is devoting time to develop your friendship with Me.

What does "the awesome mystery of a Love that encompasses you from before birth to beyond the grave" mean for us?

....

....

....

....

....

How does the certainly of God's loving Presence help us weather life's storms?

....

....

....

....

Write about a time when your friendship with God was your ultimate protection during life's storms.

....

....

....

....

READ MORE: LAMENTATIONS 3:22–26

In Weakness

The LORD gives strength to his people; the
LORD blesses his people with peace.

PSALM 29:11

BRING ME YOUR WEAKNESS, and receive My Peace. Accept yourself and your circumstances just as they are, remembering that I am sovereign over everything. Do not wear yourself out with analyzing and planning. Instead, let thankfulness and trust be your guides through this day; they will keep you close to Me. As you live in the radiance of My Presence, My Peace shines upon you. You will cease to notice how weak or strong you feel because you will be focusing on Me. The best way to get through this day is step by step with Me. Continue this intimate journey, trusting that the path you are following is headed for heaven.

> *Let thankfulness and trust be your guides through this day.*

Have you experienced God exchanging your weakness for His Peace? How?

....

....

....

....

How are "thankfulness and trust" better guides for our day than "analyzing and planning"?

....

....

....

....

....

Why is your own strength or weakness unimportant when you are focused on God?

....

....

....

....

....

READ MORE: NUMBERS 6:24–26; 13:5

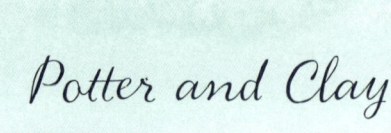

Potter and Clay

Yet, O LORD, you are our Father. We are the clay, you are the potter; we are all the work of your hand.

ISAIAH 64:8

I AM THE POTTER; you are My clay. I designed you before the foundation of the world. I arrange the events of each day to form you into this preconceived pattern. My everlasting Love is at work in every event of your life. On some days your will and Mine flow smoothly together. You tend to feel in control of your life when our wills are in harmony. On other days you feel as if you are swimming upstream, against the current of My purposes. When that happens, stop and seek My Face. The opposition you feel may be from Me, or it may be from the evil one.

Talk with Me about what you are experiencing. Let My Spirit guide you through treacherous waters. As you move through the turbulent stream with Me, let circumstances mold you into the one I desire you to be. Say *yes* to your Potter as you go through this day.

Are you ever tempted to take over the role of the Potter? Why is it better to entrust God with that role?

....

....

....

....

It's easy to see the truth of God's "everlasting love" in the joyful moments of life, but how can we see it in the less-than-joyful moments as well?

....

....

....

....

Think of a time God used an experience to shape and mold you. Write about it here.

....

....

....

....

READ MORE: PSALM 27:8; 1 JOHN 5:5–6 NKJV

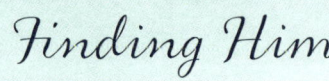

Finding Him

Therefore, holy brothers, who share in the
heavenly calling, fix your thoughts on Jesus, the
apostle and high priest whom we confess.

HEBREWS 3:1

I AM RENEWING YOUR MIND. When your thoughts flow freely, they tend to move toward problems. Your focus gets snagged on a given problem, circling round and round it in attempts to gain mastery. Your energy is drained away from other matters through this negative focus. Worst of all, you lose sight of Me.

A renewed mind is Presence-focused.

A renewed mind is Presence-focused. Train your mind to seek Me in every moment, every situation. Sometimes you can find Me in your surroundings: a lilting birdsong, a loved one's smile, golden sunlight. At other times, you must draw inward to find Me. I am always present in your spirit. Seek My Face, speak to Me, and I will light up your mind.

Do your thoughts "tend to move toward problems"? Why?

....

....

....

....

....

How have you seen the truth that "a renewed mind is Presence-focused" in your own life?

....

....

....

....

....

God is always present with us. When do you feel God most near?

....

....

....

....

....

READ MORE: PSALM 105:4; ROMANS 12:2

The Important and Unimportant

So we fix our eyes not on what is seen,
but on what is unseen. For what is seen is
temporary, but what is unseen is eternal.

2 CORINTHIANS 4:18

DO NOT SEARCH FOR SECURITY in the world you inhabit. You tend to make mental checklists of things you need to do in order to gain control of your life. If only you could check everything off your list, you could relax and be at peace. But the more you work to accomplish that goal, the more things crop up on your list. The harder you try, the more frustrated you become.

There is a better way to find security in this life. Instead of scrutinizing your checklist, focus your attention on My Presence with you. This continual contact with Me will keep you in My Peace. Moreover, I will help you sort out what is important and what is not, what needs to be done now and what does not. *Fix your eyes not on what is seen* (your circumstances), *but on what is unseen* (My Presence).

How do we get caught up in our to-do lists, finding security in what we are able to accomplish?

....

....

....

....

....

Where does our true security lie? Why?

....

....

....

....

....

Write out a prayer asking God to sift through your day, to "sort out what is important and what is not, what needs to be done now and what does not."

....

....

....

....

READ MORE: 3:1; ISAIAH 26:3 NKJV

Depending on Jesus

For we walk by faith, not by sight.

2 CORINTHIANS 5:7 NKJV

YOU CAN ACHIEVE THE VICTORIOUS LIFE through living in deep dependence on Me. People usually associate victory with success: not falling or stumbling, not making mistakes. But those who are successful in their own strength tend to go their own way, forgetting about Me. It is through problems and failure, weakness and neediness, that you learn to rely on Me.

It is a faith-walk, taken one step at a time.

True dependence is not simply asking Me to bless what you have decided to do. It is coming to Me with an open mind and heart, inviting Me to plant My desires within you. I may infuse within you a dream that seems far beyond your reach. You know that in yourself you cannot achieve such a goal. Thus begins your journey of profound reliance on Me. It is a faith-walk, taken one step at a time, leaning on Me as much as you need. This is not a path of continual success but of multiple failures. However, each failure is followed by a growth spurt, nourished by increased reliance on Me. Enjoy the blessedness of a victorious life through deepening your dependence on Me.

Have you ever asked God to bless something you've already decided to do? How did that go?

....

....

....

....

....

Are you living in true dependence on Jesus? How? Where could you lean on Him more?

....

....

....

....

....

READ MORE: PSALM 34:17–18

Transformed

You have set our iniquities before you, our
secret sins in the light of your presence.

PSALM 90:8

I WANT YOU TO BE ALL MINE, filled with the Light of My Presence. I gave everything for you by living as a man, then dying for your sins and living again. Hold back nothing from Me. Bring your most secret thoughts into the Light of My Love. Anything you bring to Me I transform and cleanse from darkness. I know everything about you, far more than you know of yourself. But I restrain My yearning to "fix" you, waiting instead for you to come to Me for help. Imagine the divine restraint this requires, for *I have all Power in heaven and on earth.*

Seek My Face with a teachable spirit. Come into My Presence with thanksgiving, desiring to be transformed.

Is there a part of your life you are holding back from the One who held nothing back from you? What would it look like to give Him everything?

....

....

....

....

....

In what ways has the Light of God's Presence transformed you?

....

....

....

....

....

What does it mean to seek God's face "with a teachable spirit"? Is your spirit teachable?

....

....

....

....

READ MORE: JOHN 12:46 NKJV; MATTHEW 28:18; PSALM 100:4

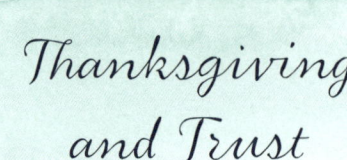

Thanksgiving and Trust

Some trust in chariots and some in horses, but
we trust in the name of the LORD our God.

PSALM 20:7

TRUST ME IN ALL YOUR THOUGHTS. I know that some thoughts are unconscious or semiconscious, and I do not hold you responsible for those. But you can direct conscious thoughts much more than you may realize. Practice thinking in certain ways—trusting Me, thanking Me—and those thoughts become more natural. Reject negative or sinful thoughts as soon as you become aware of them. Don't try to hide them from Me; confess them and leave them with Me. Go on your way lightheartedly. This method of controlling your thoughts will keep your mind in My Presence and your feet on the *path of Peace.*

Trust Me in all your thoughts.

"Trust Me in all your thoughts." Does this come easily to you? Or is it a struggle to trust God all the time?

....

....

....

....

Why is it important to "practice thinking in certain ways"?

....

....

....

....

How does thanksgiving help to strengthen our trust in God, which then leads to even greater thanksgiving?

....

....

....

....

READ MORE: 1 JOHN 1:9; LUKE 1:79

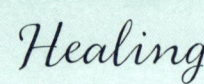

Healing

And do not be conformed to this world,
but be transformed by the renewing of your
mind, that you may prove what is that good
and acceptable and perfect will of God.

ROMANS 12:2 NKJV

RELAX IN MY HEALING, holy Presence. Allow Me to transform you through this time alone with Me. As your thoughts center more and more on Me, trust displaces fear and worry. Your mind is somewhat like a seesaw. As your trust in Me goes up, fear and worry automatically go down. Time spent with Me not only increases your trust; it also helps you discern what is important and what is not.

Energy and time are precious, limited entities. Therefore, you need to use them wisely, focusing on what is truly important. As you walk close to Me, saturating your mind with Scripture, I will show you how to spend your time and energy. *My Word is a lamp to your feet; My Presence is a Light for your path.*

What healing can we find in the "healing, holy" Presence of God?

....

....

....

....

....

In what ways do you see God seeking to transform you?

....

....

....

....

....

Resolve to saturate your mind with God's Word. Begin now by listing some of your favorite verses, and work to commit them to memory.

....

....

....

....

....

READ MORE: PSALM 52:8; EPHESIANS 5:15–16 NKJV; PSALM 119:105

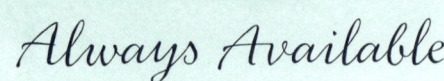

Always Available

"Though the mountains be shaken and the hills
be removed, yet my unfailing love for you will not
be shaken nor my covenant of peace be removed,"
says the LORD, who has compassion on you.

ISAIAH 54:10

I AM ALWAYS AVAILABLE TO YOU. Once you have trusted Me as your Savior, I never distance Myself from you. Sometimes you may *feel* distant from Me. Recognize that as feeling; do not confuse it with reality. The Bible is full of My promises to be with you always. As I assured Jacob, when he was journeying away from home into unknown places, *I am with you and will watch over you wherever you go.* After My resurrection, I made this promise to My followers: *Surely I am with you always, to the very end of the age.* Let these assurances of My continual Presence

> **The Bible is full of My promises to be with you always.**

fill you with Joy and Peace. No matter what you may lose in this life, you can never lose your relationship with Me.

In what ways is God always available to you?

....

....

....

....

When have you felt distant from God? Why and how is that not reality?

....

....

....

....

God's Word is filled with promises of His continued Presence in our lives. What does His Presence mean to you?

....

....

....

....

READ MORE: GENESIS 28:15; MATTHEW 28:19–20

True Joy

Splendor and majesty are before him;
strength and joy in his dwelling place.

1 CHRONICLES 16:27

REMEMBER THAT JOY is not dependent on your circumstances. Some of the world's most miserable people are those whose circumstances seem the most enviable. People who reach the top of the ladder career-wise are often surprised to find emptiness awaiting them. True Joy is a by-product of living in My Presence. Therefore you can experience it in palaces, in prisons . . . anywhere.

Do not judge a day as devoid of Joy just because it contains difficulties. Instead, concentrate on staying in communication with Me. Many of the problems that clamor for your attention will resolve themselves. Other matters you must deal with, but I will help you with them. If you make problem solving secondary to the goal of living close to Me, you can find Joy even in your most difficult days.

Even on the darkest of days, Joy is possible because of God. What are the ever-present joys in your life?

....

....

....

....

How do you define true joy? Why is it dependent upon God rather than on circumstances?

....

....

....

....

In what ways can you make problem-solving secondary to living closely with God?

....

....

....

....

....

READ MORE: HABAKKUK 3:17–19

Close to Him

And my God will meet all your needs according
to his glorious riches in Christ Jesus.

PHILIPPIANS 4:19

YOU CAN LIVE as close to Me as you choose. I set up no barriers between us; neither do I tear down barriers that you erect.

People tend to think their circumstances determine the quality of their lives. So they pour their energy into trying to control those situations. They feel happy when things are going well and sad or frustrated when things don't turn out as they'd hoped. They rarely question this correlation between their circumstances and feelings. Yet it is possible *to be content in any and every situation.*

Put more energy into trusting Me and enjoying My Presence. Don't let your well-being depend on your circumstances. Instead, connect your joy to My precious promises:

I am with you and will watch over you wherever you go. I will meet all your needs according to My glorious riches. Nothing in all creation will be able to separate you from My Love.

How close to God are you? Are there places where you have stepped away from Him?

....

....

....

....

Have you set up barriers between you and God? What do you need to do to tear down those barriers?

....

....

....

....

Read the promises of Genesis 28:15; Philippians 4:19; and Romans 8:38–39. Does your life reflect your faith in these promises? What changes might you need to make so that it does?

....

....

....

....

READ MORE: PHILIPPIANS 4:12; GENESIS 28:15; ROMANS 8:38–39

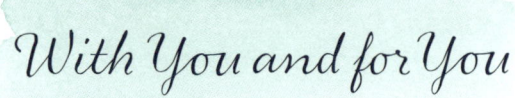

With You and for You

What, then, shall we say in response to this?
If God is for us, who can be against us?

ROMANS 8:31

I AM WITH YOU AND FOR YOU. When you decide on a course of action that is in line with My will, nothing in heaven or on earth can stop you. You may encounter many obstacles as you move toward your goal, but don't be discouraged—never give up! With My help, you can overcome any obstacle. Do not expect an easy path as you journey hand in hand with Me, but do remember that I, your *very-present Helper*, am omnipotent.

Much, much stress results from your wanting to make things happen before their times have come. One of the main ways I assert My sovereignty is in the timing of events. If you want to stay close to Me and do things My way, ask Me to show you the path forward moment by moment. Instead of dashing headlong toward your goal, let Me set the pace. Slow down, and enjoy the journey in My Presence.

How does knowing that God is with you and for you give you encouragement and strength?

....

....

....

....

Why is the path of faith not an easy journey? What obstacles have you encountered? How might you seek God's help to overcome those obstacles?

....

....

....

....

Think of a time when you pushed ahead of God's timing. What did you learn from that experience?

....

....

....

....

....

READ MORE: PSALM 46:1–3 NKJV; LUKE 1:37

Goals and God's Will

Look to the LORD and his strength;
seek his face always.

1 CHRONICLES 16:11

SAVE YOUR BEST STRIVING FOR SEEKING MY FACE. I am constantly communicating with you. To find Me and hear My voice, you must seek Me above all else. Anything that you desire more than Me becomes an idol. When you are determined to get your own way, you blot Me out of your consciousness. Instead of single-mindedly pursuing some goal, talk with Me about it. Let the Light of My Presence shine on this pursuit so that you can see it from My perspective. If the goal fits into My plans for you, I will help you reach it. If it is contrary to My will for you, I will gradually change the desire of your heart. *Seek Me first* and foremost; then the rest of your life will fall into place, piece by piece.

> *Seek Me first and foremost.*

"Anything that you desire more than Me becomes an idol." What idols do you have in your life? How do you relinquish your time, money, and thoughts to these idols? How can you turn your focus back to God?

....

....

....

....

....

....

....

"Instead of single-mindedly pursuing some goal, talk with Me about it." Are you pursuing any goals that you need to surrender to God's will? What are they?

....

....

....

....

....

....

....

READ MORE: PROVERBS 19:21 NKJV; MATTHEW 6:33

Your Strength and Song

Surely God is my salvation; I will trust and not
be afraid. The LORD, the LORD, is my strength
and my song; he has become my salvation.

ISAIAH 12:2

TRUST ME and don't be afraid, for I am your Strength and Song.
Do not let fear dissipate your energy. Instead, invest your energy
in trusting Me and singing My Song. The battle for control of
your mind is fierce, and years of worry have made you vulnerable
to the enemy. Therefore, you need to be vigilant in guarding
your thoughts. Do not despise this weakness in yourself since I
am using it to draw you closer to Me. Your constant need for Me
creates an intimacy that is well worth all the effort. You are not
alone in this struggle for your mind. My Spirit living within you
is ever ready to help in this striving. Ask Him to *control your
mind*; He will bless you with *Life and Peace*.

How are the Love and Presence of God both your strength and your song?

....

....

....

....

"Do not despise this weakness in yourself since I am using it to draw you closer to Me." Is there a weakness God has used to draw you closer to Him? What did that look like?

....

....

....

....

....

You are never alone in your struggles. How has God comforted you during a difficult time?

....

....

....

....

....

READ MORE: ROMANS 8:9; ROMANS 8:6

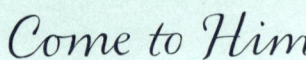

Come to Him

The Spirit and the bride say, "Come!" And
let him who hears say, "Come!" Whoever is
thirsty, let him come; and whoever wishes, let
him take the free gift of the water of life.

REVELATION 22:17

COME TO ME. *Come to Me. Come to Me.* This is My continual invitation to you, proclaimed in holy whispers. When your heart and mind are quiet, you can hear Me inviting you to draw near. Coming close to Me requires no great effort on your part; it is more like ceasing to resist the magnetic pull of My Love.

Open yourself to My loving Presence so that I may fill you with My fullness.

Open yourself to My loving Presence so that I may fill you with My fullness. I want you to experience *how wide and long and high and deep is My Love for you so that you can know My Love that surpasses knowledge.*

This vast ocean of Love cannot be measured or explained, but it can be experienced.

In what ways can you respond to God's invitation to come to Him each day?

....

....

....

....

Do you find yourself resisting "the magnetic pull" of God's love? What do you need to do to overcome this resistance?

....

....

....

....

How have you experienced God's love in your life?

....

....

....

....

READ MORE: JOHN 6:37; EPHESIANS 3:16–19

Without Complaint

Do everything without complaining or arguing, so that
you may become blameless and pure, children of God
without fault in a crooked and depraved generation,
in which you shine like stars in the universe.

PHILIPPIANS 2:14–15

YOU HAVE BEEN on a long, uphill journey, and your energy is almost spent. Though you have faltered at times, you have not let go of My hand. I am pleased with your desire to stay close to Me. There is one thing, however, that displeases Me: your tendency to complain. You may talk to Me as much as you like about the difficulty of the path we are following. I understand better than anyone else the stresses and strains that have afflicted you. You can ventilate safely to Me because talking with Me tempers your thoughts and helps you see things from My perspective.

Complaining to others is another matter altogether. It opens the door to deadly sins such as self-pity and rage. Whenever you are tempted to grumble, come to Me and talk it out. As you open up to Me, I will put My thoughts in your mind and My song in your heart.

Is complaining one of your weaknesses? What do you complain about?

....

....

....

....

....

What makes complaining to others different from complaining to God?

....

....

....

....

....

Are there complaints you need to lay before God today? Ask Him to replace your complaining thoughts with a song of rejoicing.

....

....

....

....

....

READ MORE: JEREMIAH 31:25; PSALM 40:3

Difficult Days

"So do not fear, for I am with you; do not
be dismayed, for I am your God. I will
strengthen you and help you; I will uphold
you with my righteous right hand."

ISAIAH 41:10

LEARN TO APPRECIATE difficult days. Be stimulated by the challenges you encounter along your way. As you journey through rough terrain with Me, gain confidence from your knowledge that together we can handle anything. This knowledge is comprised of three parts: your relationship with Me, promises in the Bible, and past experiences of coping successfully during hard times.

Look back on your life, and see how I have helped you through difficult days. If you are tempted to think, "Yes, but that was then, and this is now," remember who I AM! Although you and your circumstances may change dramatically, *I remain the same* throughout time and eternity. This is the basis of your confidence. In My Presence *you live and move and have your being.*

Think of a difficult day in your life. Looking back, what can you now find to appreciate in it?

....

....

....

....

It is tempting to approach difficult days on our own. How do those days— and our attitude toward them—change when we invite the power of God into them?

....

....

....

....

How does God's past faithfulness affect your walk with Him today?

....

....

....

....

....

READ MORE: PSALM 102:27; ACTS 17:27–28

Complete in Him

For the LORD God is a sun and shield; the LORD will give grace
and glory; no good thing will He withhold from those who walk
uprightly. O LORD of hosts, blessed is the man who trusts in You!

PSALM 84:11–12 NKJV

YOUR NEEDS AND MY RICHES are a perfect fit. I never meant for
you to be self-sufficient. Instead, I designed you to need Me not
only for daily bread but also for fulfillment of deep yearnings.

I carefully crafted your
longings and feelings of
incompleteness to point
you to Me. Therefore, do
not try to bury or deny
these feelings. Beware
also of trying to pacify these longings with lesser gods: people,
possessions, power.

> Come to Me in all your
> neediness, with defenses down
> and with desire to be blessed.

Come to Me in all your neediness, with defenses down and
with desire to be blessed. As you spend time in My Presence,

94

your deepest longings are fulfilled. Rejoice in your neediness, which enables you to find intimate completion in Me.

In a world that praises self-sufficiency, are you fully leaning on God?

....

....

....

....

What are the lesser gods (people, possessions, power) that tempt you away from dependence on God?

....

....

....

....

What steps can you take to more fully find yourself in Him?

....

....

....

....

READ MORE: PHILIPPIANS 4:19; COLOSSIANS 2:2–3

Slowing Down

"Martha, Martha," the Lord answered, "you are worried and upset about many things, but only one thing is needed. Mary has chosen what is better, and it will not be taken away from her."

LUKE 10:41–42

TRUST ME ENOUGH to spend ample time with Me, pushing back the demands of the day. Refuse to feel guilty about something that is so pleasing to Me, the King of the universe. Because I am omnipotent, I am able to bend time and events in your favor. You will find that you can accomplish *more* in less time after you have given yourself to Me in rich communion. Also, as you align yourself with My perspective, you can sort out what is important and what is not.

Don't fall into the trap of being constantly on the go. Many, many things people do in My Name have no value in My kingdom. To avoid doing meaningless works, stay in continual communication with Me. *I will instruct you and teach you in the way you should go; I will counsel you with My eye upon you.*

How could being "constantly on the go" become a trap, keeping us distant from God? What steps can you take to escape that trap?

....

....

....

....

....

Are "meaningless works" taking up God's space in your life? What are they?

....

....

....

....

Resolve to choose what is better, and write your commitment here.

....

....

....

....

READ MORE: HEBREWS 1:1–2; PSALM 32:8 NASB

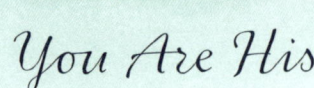

You Are His

If the LORD delights in a man's way, he makes
his steps firm; though he stumble, he will not
fall, for the LORD upholds him with his hand.

PSALM 37:23–24

YOU ARE MINE FOR ALL TIME—and beyond time, into eternity. No power can deny you your inheritance in heaven. I want you to realize how utterly secure you are! Even if you falter as you journey through life, I will never let go of your hand.

Knowing that your future is absolutely assured can free you to live abundantly today. I have prepared this day for you with the most tender concern and attention to detail. Instead of approaching the day as a blank page that you need to fill up, try living it in a responsive mode, being on the lookout for all that I am doing. This sounds easy, but it requires a deep level of trust, based on the knowledge that *My way is perfect.*

"You are Mine for all time—and beyond time, into eternity." Describe the security that truth instills in your life.

....

....

....

....

God loves us even when we fall short and make mistakes. What does this statement say about perfectionism?

....

....

....

....

God fills each day with opportunities and endless details just for you. What opportunities and details have you seen from Him today?

....

....

....

....

....

READ MORE: 1 PETER 1:3–4; PSALM 18:30

Moment by Moment

But I trust in you, O LORD; I say, "You are my God."

PSALM 31:14

TRUSTING ME is a moment-by-moment choice. My people have not always understood this truth. After I performed miracles in the wilderness, My chosen children trusted Me intensely—but only temporarily. Soon the grumbling began again, testing My patience to the utmost.

Isn't it often the same way with you? You trust Me when things go well, when you see Me working on your behalf. This type of trust flows readily within you, requiring no exertion of your will. When things go wrong, your trust-flow slows down and solidifies. You are forced to choose between trusting Me

> Trusting Me is a moment-by-moment choice.

intentionally or rebelling, resenting My ways with you. This choice constitutes a fork in the road. Stay on the path of Life with Me, enjoying My Presence. Choose to trust Me in all circumstances.

How is trusting God a moment-by-moment choice?

....

....

....

....

....

Why is it difficult to choose to keep trusting God when things go wrong?

....

....

....

....

....

"Choose to trust Me in all circumstances." What encourages you to trust God—especially when things are not going well?

....

....

....

....

....

READ MORE: EXODUS 15:22–25

Mistakes

When pride comes, then comes disgrace,
but with humility comes wisdom.

PROVERBS 11:2

DON'T BE SO HARD ON YOURSELF. I can bring good even out of your mistakes. Your finite mind tends to look backward, longing to undo decisions you have come to regret. This is a waste of time and energy, leading only to frustration. Instead of floundering in the past, release your mistakes to Me. Look to Me in trust, anticipating that My infinite creativity can weave both good choices and bad into a lovely design.

Because you are human, you will continue to make mistakes. Thinking that you should live an error-free life is symptomatic of pride. Your failures can be a source of blessing, humbling you and giving you empathy for other people in their weaknesses. Best of all, failure highlights your dependence on Me. I am able to bring beauty out of the morass of your mistakes. Trust Me, and watch to see what I will do.

"Don't be so hard on yourself. I can bring good even out of your mistakes." Are there times when you have been too hard on yourself? How has pride played a role in this?

....

....

....

....

....

What goodness have you seen God bring out of mistakes?

....

....

....

....

Are there mistakes you need to release to God? Entrust them to Him here, and ask Him to use those mistakes for your good and His glory.

....

....

....

....

READ MORE: ROMANS 8:28; MICAH 7:7

Unseen Things

Open my eyes, that I may see
wondrous things from Your law.

PSALM 119:18 NKJV

WHEN YOU APPROACH ME in stillness and in trust, you are strengthened. You need a buffer zone of silence around you in order to *focus on things that are unseen*. Since I am invisible, you must not let your senses dominate your thinking. The curse of this age is overstimulation of the senses, which blocks out awareness of the unseen world.

The tangible world still reflects My Glory to those who have eyes that see and ears that hear. Spending time alone with Me is the best way to develop seeing eyes and hearing ears. The goal is to be aware of unseen things even as you live out your life in the visible world.

What noises in your life are crowding out God?

....

....

....

....

What does it mean to have "eyes that see and ears that hear"? What changes would you like to make in order to better focus on God?

....

....

....

....

....

Write a prayer asking God to increase your awareness of the "unseen things . . . in the visible world."

....

....

....

....

....

READ MORE: 2 CORINTHIANS 4:18; ISAIAH 6:3; PSALM 130:5

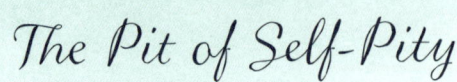

The Pit of Self-Pity

He lifted me out of the slimy pit, out of the mud and mire; he
set my feet on a rock and gave me a firm place to stand. He
put a new song in my mouth, a hymn of praise to our God.
Many will see and fear and put their trust in the LORD.

PSALM 40:2–3

SELF-PITY IS A SLIMY, BOTTOMLESS PIT. Once you fall in, you
tend to go deeper and deeper into the mire. As you slide down
those slippery walls, you are well on your way to depression, and
the darkness is profound.

Your only hope is to look up and see the Light of My Presence
shining down on you. Though the Light looks dim from your
perspective, deep in the pit, those rays of hope can reach you at
any depth. While you focus on Me in trust, you rise ever so slowly
out of the abyss of despair. Finally, you can reach up and grasp
My hand. I will pull you out into the Light again. I will gently
cleanse you, washing off the clinging mire. I will cover you with
My righteousness and walk with you down the path of Life.

How is self-pity like a pit? Is it one you have fallen into?

....

....

....

....

....

Read the words of Psalm 30:2–3. When we focus on God, what does He do for us?

....

....

....

....

....

Can we ever sink so far that God's Light cannot reach us? What does this say about the grace we should offer both ourselves and others?

....

....

....

....

READ MORE: PSALM 42:5 NASB; PSALM 147:11

Equipped for Trouble

"I have told you these things, so that in me you
may have peace. In this world you will have trouble.
But take heart! I have overcome the world."

JOHN 16:33

DO NOT LONG FOR THE ABSENCE of problems in your life. That is an unrealistic goal since *in this world you will have trouble*. You have an eternity of problem-free living reserved for you in heaven. Rejoice in that inheritance, which no one can take away from you, but do not seek your heaven on earth.

Discuss everything with Me.

Begin each day anticipating problems, asking Me to equip you for whatever difficulties you will encounter. The best equipping is My living Presence, *My hand that never lets go of yours*. Discuss everything with Me. Take a lighthearted view of trouble, seeing it as a challenge that you and I together can handle. Remember that I am on your side, and *I have overcome the world*.

Why is it better to begin the day "anticipating problems" than to expect a day free of all troubles? As we anticipate problems, what should we also do?

....

....

....

....

Read Isaiah 41:13. What promises does God offer in this verse? Are you claiming those promises? How?

....

....

....

....

....

Write out a prayer asking God to equip you for any difficulties that lay ahead.

....

....

....

....

....

READ MORE: ISAIAH 41:13; PHILIPPIANS 4:13

God with You

"The thief comes only to steal and kill and destroy;
I have come that they may have life, and have it
to the full. I am the good shepherd. The good
shepherd lays down his life for the sheep."

JOHN 10:10–11

LEARN TO ENJOY LIFE MORE. Relax, remembering that I am *God
with you*. I crafted you with enormous capacity to know Me
and enjoy My Presence. When My people wear sour faces and
walk through their lives with resigned rigidity, I am displeased.
When you walk through a day with childlike delight, savoring
every blessing, you proclaim your trust in Me, your ever-present
Shepherd. The more you focus on My Presence with you, the
more fully you can enjoy life. Glorify Me through your pleasure
in Me. Thus you proclaim My Presence to the watching world.

What does it mean that God gave up heaven to be with us?

....

....

....

....

Are you walking through your days with a sour face? How can you cultivate the childlike delight that is pleasing to God?

....

....

....

....

....

Read John 10:10–11. What kind of life did Jesus come to give? Are you embracing that life?

....

....

....

....

....

READ MORE: MATTHEW 1:23; JUDE VV. 24–25

Unconditional Love

"Greater love has no one than this, that
he lay down his life for his friends."

JOHN 15:13

REST IN ME, MY CHILD. This time devoted to Me is meant to be peaceful, not stressful. You don't have to perform in order to receive My Love. I have boundless, unconditional Love for you. How it grieves Me to see My children working for Love: trying harder and harder, yet never feeling good enough to be loved.

> *This time devoted to Me is meant to be peaceful, not stressful.*

Be careful that your devotion to Me does not become another form of works. I want you to come into My Presence joyfully and confidently. You have nothing to fear, for you wear My own righteousness. Gaze into My eyes, and you will see no condemnation, only Love and delight in the one I see. Be blessed as *My Face shines radiantly upon you, giving you Peace.*

Do you struggle to accept a love that isn't based on performance or "goodness"?

....

....

....

....

....

Have you ever found your devotion becoming a work in itself, an attempt to earn God's love?

....

....

....

....

....

What does *unconditional love* mean to you? How have you found that in God?

....

....

....

....

....

READ MORE: 2 CORINTHIANS 5:21 NKJV; ZEPHANIAH 3:17; NUMBERS 6:25–26

Through His Eyes

And hope does not disappoint us, because
God has poured out his love into our hearts
by the Holy Spirit, whom he has given us.

ROMANS 5:5

BEWARE OF SEEING YOURSELF through other people's eyes. There are several dangers to this practice. First of all, it is nearly impossible to discern what others actually think of you. Moreover, their views of you are variable: subject to each viewer's spiritual, emotional, and physical condition. The major problem with letting others define you is that it borders on idolatry. Your concern to please others dampens your desire to please Me, your Creator.

It is much more real to see yourself through *My eyes*. My gaze upon you is steady and sure, untainted by sin. Through My eyes you can see yourself as one who is deeply, eternally loved. Rest in My loving gaze, and you will receive deep Peace. Respond to My loving Presence by *worshiping Me in spirit and in truth*.

Why is seeing ourselves through other people's eyes such a danger to our relationship with God?

....

....

....

....

Has pleasing people become an idol in your life? How can you return your focus to God?

....

....

....

....

....

How does God see you? What verses reveal this truth to you?

....

....

....

....

....

READ MORE: HEBREWS 11:6; JOHN 4:23–24

Understood and Loved

Those who look to him are radiant; their
faces are never covered with shame.

PSALM 34:5

BASK IN THE LUXURY of being fully understood and unconditionally loved. Dare to see yourself as I see you: radiant in My
righteousness, cleansed by My blood. I view you as the one I created
you to be, the one you will be in actuality when heaven becomes
your home. It is My Life within you that is changing you *from glory
to glory*. Rejoice in this mysterious miracle! Thank Me continually for the amazing gift of My Spirit within you.

> Dare to see yourself as I see you: radiant in My righteousness, cleansed by My blood.

Try to depend on
the help of the Spirit as you go through this day of life. Pause
briefly from time to time so you can consult with this Holy One
inside you. He will not force you to do His bidding, but He will

116

guide you as you give Him space in your life. Walk along this wondrous way of collaboration with My Spirit.

Why is "being fully understood and unconditionally loved" such a luxury in today's world?

....

....

....

How does knowing that God sees us as He created us to be offer reassurance during those times when we sin?

....

....

....

....

How is God working in your life to transform you into who He created you to be?

....

....

....

....

READ MORE: 2 CORINTHIANS 5:21; 2 CORINTHIANS 3:18 NKJV; GALATIANS 5:25

Filling the Emptiness

"Blessed are the poor in spirit, for theirs is the
kingdom of heaven. . . . Blessed are those who hunger
and thirst for righteousness, for they will be filled."

MATTHEW 5:3, 6

COME TO ME with your gaping emptiness, knowing that in Me
you are complete. As you rest quietly in My Presence, My Light
within you grows brighter and brighter. Facing the emptiness
inside you is simply the prelude to being filled with My fullness.
Therefore, rejoice on those days when you drag yourself out of
bed, feeling sluggish and inadequate. Tell yourself that this is a
perfect day to depend on Me in childlike trust. If you persevere
in this dependence as you go through the day, you will discover
at bedtime that Joy and Peace have become your companions.
You may not realize at what point they joined you on your journey, but you will feel the beneficial effects of their presence. The
perfect end to such a day is a doxology of gratitude. I am He
from whom all blessings flow!

How does knowing that God will fill up our "gaping emptiness" offer comfort?

....

....

....

....

....

How does stepping into the Presence of the Lord fill that emptiness?

....

....

....

....

What difference would it make to approach your day with childlike trust in Him? What practical steps could you take to encourage that childlike trust?

....

....

....

....

....

READ MORE: 2 CORINTHIANS 4:6; COLOSSIANS 2:9–10; PSALM 150:6

Saturated in Grace

But the LORD said to Samuel, "Do not consider his appearance
or his height, for I have rejected him. The LORD does not
look at the things man looks at. Man looks at the outward
appearance, but the LORD looks at the heart."

1 SAMUEL 16:7

LET ME BLESS YOU with My grace and Peace. Open your heart
and mind to receive all that I have for you. Do not be ashamed
of your emptiness. Instead, view it as the optimal condition for
being filled with My Peace.

It is easy to touch up your outward appearance, to look as if
you have it all together. Your attempts to look good can fool most
people. But I see straight through you, into the depths of your
being. There is no place for pretense in your relationship with Me.
Rejoice in the relief of being fully understood. Talk with Me about
your struggles and feelings of inadequacy. Little by little, I will
transform your weaknesses into strengths. Remember that your
relationship with Me is saturated in grace. Therefore, *nothing that
you do or don't do can separate you from My Presence.*

How do we sometimes touch up our outward appearance in order to convince the world that we have it all together?

....

....

....

....

....

"I see straight through you, into the depths of your being." Does this truth bring you comfort, fear, or both?

....

....

....

....

....

"Your relationship with Me is saturated in grace." How important is this reality to your relationship with God?

....

....

....

....

....

READ MORE: ROMANS 8:38–39

The Adventure of Today

"For I am the LORD, your God, who takes
hold of your right hand and says to
you, Do not fear; I will help you."

ISAIAH 41:13

GIVE YOURSELF FULLY to the adventure of today. Walk boldly along the path of Life, relying on your ever-present Companion. You have every reason to be confident because My Presence accompanies you all the days of your life—and onward into eternity.

Do not give in to fear or worry, those robbers of abundant living. Trust Me enough to face problems as they come, rather than trying to anticipate them. *Fix your eyes on Me, the Author and Perfecter of your faith*, and many difficulties on the road ahead will vanish before you reach them. Whenever you start to feel afraid, remember that *I am holding you by your right hand*. Nothing can separate you from My Presence!

What adventures can you find in this day? Are you ready to "give yourself fully" to them?

....

....

....

....

Have fear and worry ever robbed you of the abundant life? How?

....

....

....

....

"Nothing can separate you from My Presence!" How does this truth give you courage as you face the adventures and challenges of today?

....

....

....

....

READ MORE: PSALM 48:14; HEBREWS 12:2

Wait, Trust, Hope

Wait for the LORD; be strong and take
heart and wait for the LORD.

PSALM 27:14

WAITING, TRUSTING, AND HOPING are intricately connected, like golden strands interwoven to form a strong chain. Trusting is the central strand because it is the response from My children that I desire the most. Waiting and hoping embellish the central strand and strengthen the chain that connects you to Me. Waiting for Me to work, with your eyes on Me, is evidence that you really do trust Me. If you mouth the words "I trust You" while anxiously trying to make things go your way, your words ring hollow. Hoping is future-directed, connecting you to your inheritance in heaven. However, the benefits of hope fall fully on you in the present.

> *You can wait expectantly, in hopeful trust.*

Because you are Mine, you don't just pass time in your waiting. You can wait expectantly, in hopeful trust. Keep your "antennae" out to pick up even the faintest glimmer of My Presence.

How are waiting, trusting, and hoping intricately connected?

....

....

....

....

How is hoping connected to your inheritance in heaven?

....

....

....

....

What does it mean to "wait expectantly"? How can you wait with expectation?

....

....

....

....

READ MORE: JOHN 14:1; HEBREWS 6:18–20

Loving Others

Your love, O LORD, reaches to the heavens,
your faithfulness to the skies.

PSALM 36:5

LEARN TO RELATE to others through My Love rather than yours. Your human love is ever so limited, full of flaws and manipulation. My loving Presence, which always enfolds you, is available to bless others as well as you. Instead of trying harder to help people through your own paltry supplies, become aware of My unlimited supply, which is accessible to you continually. Let My Love envelop your outreach to other people.

Many of My precious children have fallen prey to burnout. A better description of their condition might be "drainout." Countless interactions with needy people have drained them, without their conscious awareness. You are among these weary ones, who are like wounded soldiers needing R & R. Take time to rest in the Love-Light of My Presence. I will gradually restore to you the energy that you have lost over the years. *Come to Me, all you who are weary and burdened, and you will find rest for your souls.*

How does relating to others through God's love differ from relating to them through your own love? What changes might you need to make in the way you relate to others?

....

....

....

....

Are you weary from "drainout" in your life? How can turning to God restore your lost energy?

....

....

....

Read Matthew 11:28–29. Lay your burdens before Him. Journal here about your time together.

....

....

....

READ MORE: EXODUS 33:14; MATTHEW 11:28–29

Your Path

He has showed you, O man, what is good. And what
does the LORD require of you? To act justly and to
love mercy and to walk humbly with your God.

MICAH 6:8

STAY ON THE HIGH ROAD WITH ME. Many voices clamor for your
attention, trying to divert you to another path. But I have called
you to walk ever so closely with Me, soaking in My Presence, living in My Peace. This is My unique
design for you, planned before the
world began.

*Stay on the high
road with Me.*

I have called each of My children to a different path, distinctly
designed for that one. Do not let anyone convince you that his
path is the only right way. And be careful not to extol your path
as superior to another's way. What I require of you is *to act
justly, to love mercy, and to walk humbly with Me*—wherever
I lead.

128

What distractions pull you onto a path other than God's? How can you stand strong against their pull?

....

....

....

....

Read the promises of Ephesians 2:10. What does this reveal about the path God has prepared for each of His children?

....

....

....

....

It's easy to fall into the trap of comparing your own path to that of others. Why is that not what God wants you to do?

....

....

....

....

....

READ MORE: JOHN 14:27 NKJV; EPHESIANS 2:10

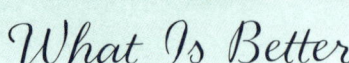

What Is Better

The fig tree forms its early fruit; the blossoming
vines spread their fragrance. Arise, come, my
darling; my beautiful one, come with me.

SONG OF SONGS 2:13

COME AWAY WITH ME for a while. The world, with its nonstop demands, can be put on hold. Most people put *Me* on hold, rationalizing that someday they will find time to focus on Me. But the longer people push Me into the background of their lives, the harder it is for them to find Me.

You live among people who glorify busyness; they have made time a tyrant that controls their lives. Even those who know Me as Savior tend to march to the tempo of the world. They have bought into the illusion that more is always better: more meetings, more programs, more activity.

I have called you to follow Me on a solitary path, making time alone with Me your highest priority and deepest Joy. It is a pathway largely unappreciated and often despised. However, *you have chosen the better thing, which will never be taken away from you.* Moreover, as you walk close to Me, I can bless others through you.

"Come away with Me for a while." When was the last time you stepped away from the world to be with God? What keeps you from stepping away with Him more often?

....

....

....

Are you someone who glorifies busyness? How can you remove the tyranny of time from your relationship with God?

....

....

....

"Mary has chosen what is better, and it will not be taken away from her" (Luke 10:42). How can you choose what is better?

....

....

....

READ MORE: LUKE 10:41–42

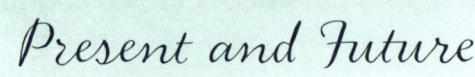

Present and Future

We have this hope as an anchor for the
soul, firm and secure. It enters the inner
sanctuary behind the curtain.

HEBREWS 6:19

HEAVEN IS both present and future. As you walk along your life-path holding My hand, you are already in touch with the essence of heaven: nearness to Me. You can also find many hints of heaven along your pathway because the earth is radiantly alive with My Presence. Shimmering sunshine awakens your heart, gently reminding you of My brilliant Light. Birds and flowers, trees and skies evoke praises to My holy Name. Keep your eyes and ears fully open as you journey with Me.

At the end of your life-path is an entrance to heaven. Only I know when you will reach that destination, but I am preparing you for it each step of the way. The absolute certainty of your heavenly home gives you Peace and Joy to help you along your journey. You know that you will reach your home in My perfect timing: not one moment too soon or too late. Let the hope of heaven encourage you as you walk along the path of Life with Me.

How can heaven be "both present and future"? How have you seen this truth in your own life?

....

....

....

....

Write about a time when you experienced the nearness of God.

....

....

....

....

How does "the hope of heaven encourage you as you walk along the path of Life"?

....

....

....

READ MORE: 1 CORINTHIANS 15:20–23

Nothing to Fear

For this God is our God for ever and ever;
he will be our guide even to the end.

PSALM 48:14

I AM YOURS FOR ALL ETERNITY. *I am the Alpha and the Omega: the One who is and was and is to come.* The world you inhabit is a place of constant changes—more than your mind can absorb without going into shock. Even the body you inhabit is changing relentlessly in spite of modern science's attempts to prolong youth and life indefinitely. *I, however, am the same yesterday and today and forever.*

Because I never change, your relationship with Me provides a rock-solid foundation for your life. I will never leave your side. When you move on from this life to the next, My Presence beside you will shine brighter with each step. You have nothing to fear because I am with you for all time and throughout eternity.

Are there worrisome changes happening in your life, in the world? What are they?

....

....

....

....

Is your life built on the rock-solid foundation of God? Or are you standing on shifting sand?

....

....

....

....

How does knowing that God is always with you and will never leave you affect the way you approach the risks, troubles, and challenges of each day?

....

....

....

....

....

READ MORE: REVELATION 1:8; HEBREWS 13:8; PSALM 102:25–27

Pleasing Him

Trust in him at all times, O people; pour out
your hearts to him, for God is our refuge.

PSALM 62:8

I AM PLEASED WITH YOU, MY CHILD. Allow yourself to become fully aware of My pleasure shining upon you. You don't have to perform well in order to receive My Love. In fact, a performance focus will pull you away from Me, toward some sort of Pharisaism. This can be a subtle form of idolatry: worshiping your own good works. It can also be a source of deep discouragement when your works don't measure up to your expectations.

> *The Light of My Love shines on you continually.*

Shift your focus from your performance to My radiant Presence. The Light of My Love shines on you continually, regardless of your feelings or behavior. Your responsibility is to be receptive to this unconditional Love. Thankfulness and trust are your primary receptors. Thank Me for everything; *trust in Me at all times*. These simple disciplines will keep you open to My loving Presence.

Do you ever find yourself "worshiping your own good works"? How is this a form of idolatry?

....

....

....

"The Light of My Love shines on you continually, regardless of your feelings or behavior." What does this say about what we must do to be pleasing to God?

....

....

....

Read Psalm 62:8. How is your trust in Him no matter the circumstances pleasing to God?

....

....

....

READ MORE: EPHESIANS 2:8–9; EPHESIANS 3:16–19

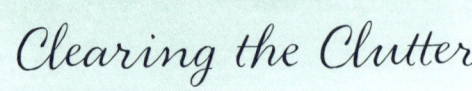

Clearing the Clutter

"But seek first his kingdom and his righteousness, and all these things will be given to you as well."

MATTHEW 6:33

Do NOT BE WEIGHED DOWN by the clutter in your life: lots of little chores to do sometime, in no particular order. If you focus too much on these petty tasks, trying to get them all out of the way, you will discover that they are endless. They can eat up as much time as you devote to them.

Remember that your ultimate goal is living close to Me.

Instead of trying to do all your chores at once, choose the ones that need to be done today. Let the rest slip into the background of your mind so I can be in the forefront of your awareness. Remember that your ultimate goal is living close to Me, being responsive to My initiatives. I can communicate with you most readily when your mind is uncluttered and turned toward Me. Seek My Face continually throughout this day. Let My Presence bring order to your thoughts, infusing Peace into your entire being.

What daily clutter weighs you down?

....

....

....

....

What is our ultimate life goal? Is it to clear away all the chores and tasks? Or is it to live close to Him? How do we do that?

....

....

....

....

Spend some time in prayer, allowing God to "bring order to your thoughts" and infuse you with His Peace. What did your time alone with Him reveal about your priorities?

....

....

....

READ MORE: PROVERBS 16:3; PSALM 27:8 NKJV; ISAIAH 26:3 NKJV

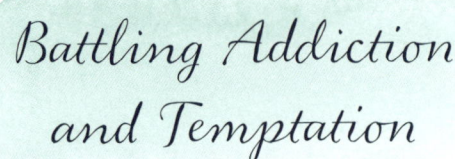

Battling Addiction and Temptation

Then Peter got down out of the boat, walked
on the water and came toward Jesus. But
when he saw the wind, he was afraid and,
beginning to sink, cried out, "Lord, save me!"

MATTHEW 14:29–30

MY FACE IS SHINING UPON YOU, beaming out *Peace that transcends understanding.* You are surrounded by a sea of problems, but you are face to Face with Me, your Peace. As long as you focus on Me, you are safe. If you gaze too long at the myriad problems around you, you will sink under the weight of your burdens. When you start to sink, simply call out, "Help me, Jesus!" and I will lift you up.

The closer you live to Me, the safer you are. Circumstances around you are undulating, and there are treacherous-looking waves in the distance. *Fix your eyes on Me*, the One who never changes. By the time those waves reach you, they will have shrunk to proportions of My design. I am always beside you, helping you face *today's* waves. The future is a phantom, seeking to spook you. Laugh at the future! Stay close to Me.

What "myriad problems" are causing you to stumble?

....

....

....

....

Do you call for Jesus to help you when you are sinking? Or do you try to lift yourself above the waves?

....

....

....

....

Write out a prayer asking Jesus to help you keep your eyes fixed on Him.

....

....

....

....

READ MORE: PHILIPPIANS 4:7; HEBREWS 12:2

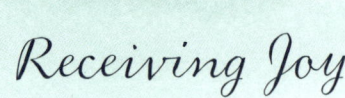

Receiving Joy

"Be still, and know that I am God; I will be exalted among the nations, I will be exalted in the earth."

PSALM 46:10

DO NOT HESITATE TO RECEIVE JOY FROM ME, for I bestow it on you abundantly. The more you rest in My Presence, the more freely My blessings flow into you. In the Light of My Love, you are gradually *transformed from glory to glory*. It is through spending time with Me that you realize *how wide and long and high and deep is My Love for you.*

> *Do not hesitate to receive Joy from Me.*

Sometimes the relationship I offer you seems too good to be true. I pour My very Life into you, and all you have to do is receive Me. In a world characterized by working and taking, the admonition to rest and receive seems too easy. There is a close connection between receiving and believing: As you trust Me more and more, you are able to receive Me and My blessings abundantly. *Be still, and know that I am God.*

Have you ever found yourself hesitating to receive God's Joy? Why?

....

....

....

....

....

"I pour My very Life into you, and all you have to do is receive Me." Why is the receiving sometimes so very hard?

....

....

....

....

....

What connection do you find between joy and stillness in His presence?

....

....

....

....

....

READ MORE: 2 CORINTHIANS 3:18 NASB; EPHESIANS 3:17–19

A Continual Gift of Peace

Let us then approach the throne of grace with
confidence, so that we may receive mercy and
find grace to help us in our time of need.

HEBREWS 4:16

PEACE IS MY CONTINUAL GIFT TO YOU. It flows abundantly from My throne of grace. Just as the Israelites could not store up manna for the future but had to gather it daily, so it is with My Peace. The day-by-day collecting of manna kept My people aware of their dependence on Me. Similarly, I give you sufficient Peace for the present when you come to me *by prayer and petition with thanksgiving.* If I gave you permanent Peace, independent of My Presence, you might fall into the trap of self-sufficiency. May that never be!

I have designed you to need Me moment by moment. As your awareness of your neediness increases, so does your realization of My abundant sufficiency. *I can meet every one of your needs* without draining My resources at all. *Approach My throne of grace with bold confidence,* receiving My Peace with a thankful heart.

How is "the day-by-day collecting of manna" similar to the moment-by-moment flow of God's Peace?

....

....

....

....

Have you seen the truth of God's "abundant sufficiency" in your own life?

....

....

....

....

God invites you to "approach [His] throne of grace with bold confidence." What does that gift mean to you and your relationship with Him?

....

....

....

....

READ MORE: EXODUS 16:15–16, 19; PHILIPPIANS 4:6–7, 19

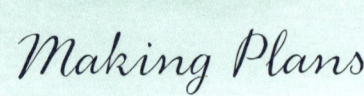

Making Plans

Many are the plans in a man's heart, but
it is the LORD's purpose that prevails.

PROVERBS 19:21

I AM YOUR LORD! Seek Me as Friend and Lover of your soul, but remember that I am also King of kings—sovereign over all. You can make some plans as you gaze into the day that stretches out before you. But you need to hold those plans tentatively, anticipating that I may have other ideas. The most important thing to determine is what to do right now. Instead of scanning the horizon of your life, looking for things that need to be done, concentrate on the task before you and the One who never leaves your side. Let everything else fade into the background. This will unclutter your mind, allowing Me to occupy more and more of your consciousness.

I will guide you step by step as you bend your will to Mine.

Trust Me to show you what to do when you have finished what you are doing now. I will guide you step by step as you bend your will to Mine. Thus you stay close to Me on the *path of Peace*.

In what ways is God the Friend, Lover of your soul, and King of kings in your life?

....

....

....

How do each of those roles affect the plans we make for ourselves? What do these roles tell us about God's plans for us?

....

....

....

....

"You need to hold those plans tentatively, anticipating that I may have other ideas." How might interruptions to your plans be part of God's divine plan?

....

....

....

....

READ MORE: REVELATION 17:14; LUKE 1:79

God Speaks

The heavens declare the glory of God; the skies proclaim
the work of his hands. Day after day they pour forth
speech; night after night they display knowledge.

PSALM 19:1–2

I SPEAK TO YOU CONTINUALLY. My nature is to communicate, though not always in words. I fling glorious sunsets across the sky, day after day after day. I speak in the faces and voices of loved ones. I caress you with a gentle breeze that refreshes and delights you. I speak softly in the depths of your spirit, where I have taken up residence.

You can find Me in each moment, when you have eyes that see and ears that hear. Ask My Spirit to sharpen your spiritual eyesight and hearing. I rejoice each time you discover My Presence. Practice looking and listening for Me during quiet intervals. Gradually you will find Me in more and more of your moments. *You will seek Me and find Me, when you seek Me above all else.*

When do you feel closest to God?

....

....

....

....

....

Read the words of Psalm 19:1–2. What message are the heavens proclaiming to you about their Creator?

....

....

....

....

....

"You can find Me in each moment." Where is God in this moment?

....

....

....

....

....

READ MORE: PSALM 8:1–4; 1 CORINTHIANS 6:19; JEREMIAH 29:13

In the Maelstrom

But now, this is what the LORD says—he who created you,
O Jacob, he who formed you, O Israel: "Fear not, for I have
redeemed you; I have summoned you by name; you are mine."

ISAIAH 43:1

FIND ME in the midst of the maelstrom. Sometimes events whirl around you so quickly that they become a blur. Whisper My Name in recognition that I am still with you. Without skipping a beat in the activities that occupy you, you find strength and Peace through praying My Name. Later, when the happenings have run their course, you can talk with Me more fully.

> *Accept each day just as it comes to you.*

Accept each day just as it comes to you. Do not waste your time and energy wishing for a different set of circumstances. Instead, trust Me enough to yield to My design and purposes. Remember that nothing can separate you from My loving Presence; *you are Mine.*

Are you able to find God "in the midst of the maelstrom"? Where is He always?

....

....

....

....

....

Are you able to accept each day just as it is? Or do you struggle to bend it to your own will?

....

....

....

....

....

Write out a prayer entrusting your life to God's "design and purposes."

....

....

....

....

....

READ MORE: PHILIPPIANS 2:9–11; 29:11

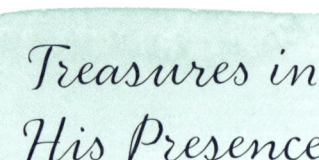

Treasures in His Presence

You have filled my heart with greater joy
than when their grain and new wine abound.
I will lie down and sleep in peace, for you
alone, O LORD, make me dwell in safety.

PSALM 4:7–8

AS YOU SIT QUIETLY IN MY PRESENCE, let Me fill your heart and mind with thankfulness. This is the most direct way to achieve a thankful stance. If your mind needs a focal point, gaze at My Love poured out for you on the cross. Remember that *nothing in heaven or on earth can separate you from that Love.* This remembrance builds a foundation of gratitude in you, a foundation that circumstances cannot shake.

As you go through this day, look for tiny treasures strategically placed along the way. I lovingly go before you and plant little pleasures to brighten your day. Look carefully for them, and pluck them one by one. When you reach the end of the day, you will have gathered a lovely bouquet. Offer it up to Me with a grateful heart. Receive My Peace as you lie down to sleep, with thankful thoughts playing a lullaby in your mind.

"If your mind needs a focal point, gaze at My Love poured out for you on the cross." What thoughts fill your mind as you focus on the love poured out on the cross?

....

....

....

What "tiny treasures" has God placed in your path today? Why are these much more than tiny treasures?

....

....

....

Take a few moments today to sit quietly in His Presence. Allow Him to fill your heart and mind with thankfulness. Record your thoughts here.

....

....

....

READ MORE: ROMANS 8:38–39; 1 CORINTHIANS 3:11

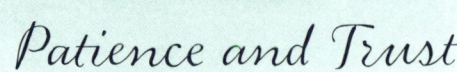

Patience and Trust

Then Jesus said, "Did I not tell you that if you believed, you would see the glory of God?"

JOHN 11:40

MY PLAN FOR YOUR LIFE is unfolding before you. Sometimes the road you are traveling seems blocked, or it opens up so painfully slowly that you must hold yourself back. Then, when time is right, the way before you suddenly clears—through no effort of your own. What you have longed for and worked for I present to you freely, as pure gift. You feel awed by the ease with which I operate in the world, and you glimpse *My Power and My Glory.*

My plan for your life is unfolding before you.

Do not fear your weakness, for it is the stage on which My Power and Glory perform most brilliantly. As you persevere along the path I have prepared for you, depending on My strength to sustain you, expect to see miracles—and you will.

Miracles are not always visible to the naked eye, but those who *live by faith* can see them clearly. *Living by faith, rather than sight*, enables you to see My Glory.

How are both patience and trust essential when we are waiting on God's plan to unfold?

....

....

....

Are you tempted to take matters into your own hands—to hurry God's plans along? How does this usually work out for you?

....

....

....

Write about a time when you saw the power of God's perfect timing at work in your life or in someone else's.

....

....

....

....

READ MORE: PSALM 63:2–5; 2 CORINTHIANS 5:7

Weighed Down

I have seen you in the sanctuary and
beheld your power and your glory.

PSALM 63:2

YOU ARE FEELING WEIGHED DOWN by a plethora of problems, both big and small. They seem to require more and more of your attention, but you must not give in to those demands. When the difficulties in your life feel as if they're closing in on you, break free by spending quality time with Me. You need to remember who I AM in all My Power and Glory. Then humbly bring Me your prayers and petitions. Your problems will pale when you view them in the Light of My Presence. You can learn to *be joyful in Me, your Savior,* even in the midst of adverse circumstances. Rely on Me, *your Strength; I make your feet like the feet of a deer, enabling you to go on the heights.*

Are there troubles or worries weighing you down? What are they? How much of your attention do they consume?

....

....

What happens to troubles and worries when we lay them before Jesus?

....

....

Think of a deer standing firm upon the heights, as described in Habakkuk 3. Are you allowing God to make you as sure-footed as that deer?

....

....

READ MORE: EXODUS 3:14; HABAKKUK 3:17–19

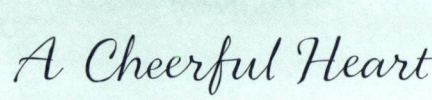

A Cheerful Heart

A cheerful heart is good medicine, but a
crushed spirit dries up the bones.

PROVERBS 17:22

IT IS GOOD THAT YOU RECOGNIZE YOUR WEAKNESS. That keeps you looking to Me, your Strength. Abundant life is not necessarily health and wealth; it is living in continual dependence on Me. Instead of trying to fit this day into a preconceived mold, relax and be on the lookout for what I am doing. This mind-set will free you to enjoy Me and to find what I have planned for you to do. This is far better than trying to make things go according to your own plan.

Lighten up and laugh with Me.

Don't take yourself so seriously. Lighten up and laugh with Me. You have Me on your side, so what are you worried about? I can equip you to do absolutely anything, as long as it is My will. The more difficult your day, the more I yearn to help you. Anxiety wraps you up in yourself, trapping you in your own thoughts. When you look to Me and whisper My Name, you break free and receive My help. Focus on Me, and you will find Peace in My Presence.

What weaknesses do you see in yourself? Why is it good to recognize those weaknesses?

....

....

....

Is there an area where you need to lighten up, to laugh, and to trust God more?

....

....

....

....

"Relax and be on the lookout for what I am doing." What do you see God doing today?

....

....

....

....

READ MORE: PHILIPPIANS 4:13 AMP

His Love

Let your face shine on your servant;
save me in your unfailing love.

PSALM 31:16

I LOVE YOU regardless of how well you are performing. Sometimes you feel uneasy, wondering if you are doing enough to be worthy of My Love. No matter how exemplary your behavior, the answer to that question will always be no. Your performance and My Love are totally different issues, which you need to sort out. *I love you with an everlasting Love* that flows out from eternity without limits or conditions. *I have clothed you in My robe of righteousness,* and this is an eternal transaction: Nothing and no one can reverse it. Therefore, your accomplishment as a Christian has no bearing on My Love for you. Even your ability to assess how well you are doing on a given day is flawed. Your limited human perspective and the condition of your body, with its mercurial variations, distort your evaluations.

Bring your performance anxiety to Me, and receive in its

place *My unfailing Love.* Try to stay conscious of My loving Presence with you in all that you do, and I will direct your steps.

So much of this world's approval and love is based on performance, yet God promises to love us regardless. What does this truth mean to you?

....

....

....

"I love you with an everlasting Love that flows out from eternity without limits or conditions." How does the knowledge of God's endless love change your thinking about yourself?

....

....

....

....

Write out a prayer praising God for His unfailing love.

....

....

....

....

READ MORE: JEREMIAH 31:3; ISAIAH 61:10; PSALM 107:8

Safe and Secure

"I give them eternal life, and they shall never perish; no one can snatch them out of my hand. My Father, who has given them to me, is greater than all; no one can snatch them out of my Father's hand."

JOHN 10:28–29

I WANT YOU TO KNOW how safe and secure you are in My Presence. That is a fact, totally independent of your feelings. You are on your way to heaven; nothing can prevent you from reaching that destination. There you will see Me face to Face, and your Joy will be off the charts by any earthly standards. Even now, you are never separated from Me, though you must see Me through eyes of faith. I will walk with you till the end of time and onward into eternity.

Although My Presence is a guaranteed promise, that does not necessarily change your feelings. When you forget I am with you, you may experience loneliness or fear. It is through awareness of My Presence that Peace displaces negative feelings. Practice the discipline of walking consciously with Me through each day.

How have you found safety and security in God's Presence? What steps can you take to slow down?

....

....

....

....

....

In John 10, Jesus promises that no one can snatch you out of His Father's hand (v. 29). What does this promise mean to you in light of troubles, mistakes, worries, and fears?

....

....

....

....

....

How can you practice the discipline of walking consciously with God every day?

....

....

....

....

READ MORE: 1 CORINTHIANS 13:12; PSALM 29:11

Time for God

There is a time for everything, and a season
for every activity under heaven.

ECCLESIASTES 3:1

WAIT PATIENTLY WITH ME while I bless you. Don't rush into My Presence with time-consciousness gnawing at your mind. I dwell in timelessness: *I am, I was, I will always be.* For you, time is a protection; you're a frail creature who can handle only twenty-four-hour segments of life. Time can also be a tyrant, ticking away relentlessly in your mind. Learn to master time, or it will be your master.

Though you are a time-bound creature, seek to meet Me in timelessness. As you focus on My Presence, the demands of time and tasks will diminish. *I will bless you and keep you, making My Face shine upon you graciously, giving you Peace.*

Do you struggle with rushing your time with God? Why? How can you address this?

....

....

....

....

....

How is time both a "protection" and a "tyrant"? How can we "learn to master time"?

....

....

....

....

Ecclesiastes 3:1 tells us that there is a time for everything. When is your time for God?

....

....

....

....

READ MORE: MICAH 7:7; REVELATION 1:8; NUMBERS 6:24–26

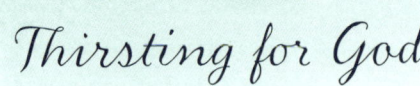

Thirsting for God

As the deer pants for streams of water, so my soul
pants for you, O God. My soul thirsts for God, for
the living God. When can I go and meet with God?

PSALM 42:1–2

SEEK MY FACE, and you will find all that you have longed for. The deepest yearnings of your heart are for intimacy with Me. I know because I designed you to desire Me. Do not feel guilty about taking time to be still in My Presence. You are simply responding to the tugs of divinity within you. I made you in My image, and I hid heaven in your heart. Your yearning for Me is a form of homesickness: longing for your true home in heaven.

Do not be afraid to be different from other people. The path I have called you to travel is exquisitely right for you. The more closely you follow My leading, the more fully I can develop your gifts. To follow Me wholeheartedly, you must relinquish your desire to please other people. However, your closeness to Me will bless others by enabling you to shine brightly in this dark world.

Do you find yourself longing for heaven, for a home with God? Why?

....

....

....

....

....

Are you afraid to be different? What does God say about being different?

....

....

....

....

....

Why must we surrender our desire to please others? How might that desire interfere with your closeness to God?

....

....

....

....

....

READ MORE: 34:5; PHILIPPIANS 2:15

In Adversity

He who dwells in the shelter of the Most High
will rest in the shadow of the Almighty.

PSALM 91:1

EXPECT TO ENCOUNTER ADVERSITY in your life, remembering that you live in a deeply fallen world. Stop trying to find a way that circumvents difficulties. The main problem with an easy life is that it masks your need for Me. When you became a Christian, I infused My very Life into you, empowering you to live on a supernatural plane by depending on Me.

Anticipate coming face to face with impossibilities: situations totally beyond your ability to handle. This awareness of your inadequacy is not something you should try to evade. It is precisely where I want you—the best place to encounter Me in *My Glory and Power.* When you see armies of problems marching toward you, cry out to Me! Allow Me to fight for you. Watch Me working on your behalf, as you *rest in the shadow of My Almighty Presence.*

In times of adversity, how does knowing that you are empowered by God help you carry on?

....

....

....

....

....

How might an awareness of your inadequacy better enable you to encounter the glory and power of God?

....

....

....

....

Think of a time God fought on your behalf, and write out a prayer of praise to Him.

....

....

....

....

READ MORE: JOB 5:7; REVELATION 19:1

The Freedom of Forgiveness

There is no fear in love. But perfect love drives
out fear, because fear has to do with punishment.
The one who fears is not made perfect in love.

1 JOHN 4:18

WALK WITH ME in the freedom of forgiveness. The path we follow together is sometimes steep and slippery. If you carry a burden of guilt on your back, you are more likely to stumble and fall. At your request, I will remove the heavy load from you and bury it at the foot of the cross. When I unburden you, you are undeniably free! Stand up straight and tall in My Presence so that no one can place more burdens on your back. Look into My Face and feel the warmth of My Love-Light shining upon you. It is this unconditional Love that frees you from both fears and sins.

Spend time basking in the Light of My Presence.

Spend time basking in the Light of My Presence. As you come to know Me more and more intimately, you grow increasingly free.

What does the "freedom of forgiveness" mean to you?

....

....

....

....

How has guilt caused you to stumble and fall? Is that God's desire for you?

....

....

....

....

How does God's unconditional love free us? Have you fully embraced that freedom?

....

....

....

....

READ MORE: PSALM 68:19; 1 JOHN 1:7–9

Joy in His Presence

Surely you have granted him eternal blessings and
made him glad with the joy of your presence.

PSALM 21:6

No matter what your circumstances may be, you can find
Joy in My Presence. On some days, Joy is generously strewn
along your life-path, glistening in the sunlight. On days like
that, being content is as simple as breathing the next breath or
taking the next step. Other days are overcast and gloomy; you
feel the strain of the journey, which seems endless. Dull gray
rocks greet your gaze and cause your feet to ache. Yet Joy is still
attainable. *Search for it as for hidden treasure.*

Begin by remembering that I have created this day; it is not
a chance occurrence. Recall that I am present with you whether
you sense My Presence or not. Then, start talking with Me about
whatever is on your mind. Rejoice in the fact that I understand
you perfectly and I know exactly what you are experiencing.
As you continue communicating with Me, your mood will

gradually lighten. Awareness of My marvelous Companionship can infuse Joy into the grayest day.

How does remembering that God is the Author of our days change the way you think about obstacles and challenges?

....

....

....

....

So often we reserve talking to God for the loftier things. What might change if you chose to talk to Him about everything?

....

....

....

....

"Awareness of My marvelous Companionship can infuse Joy into the grayest day." How have you been aware of God's Presence today?

....

....

....

READ MORE: PROVERBS 2:4; COLOSSIANS 1:16 NKJV

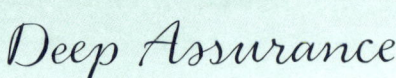

Deep Assurance

Let them give thanks to the LORD for his
unfailing love and his wonderful deeds for
men. Let them sacrifice thank offerings
and tell of his works with songs of joy.

PSALM 107:21–22

REST IN THE DEEP ASSURANCE of My unfailing Love. Let your body, mind, and spirit relax in My Presence. Release into My care anything that is troubling you so that you can focus your full attention on Me. Be awed by the vast dimensions of My Love for you: *wider, longer, higher, and deeper* than anything you know. Rejoice that this marvelous Love is yours forever!

The best response to this glorious gift is a life steeped in thankfulness. Every time you thank Me, you acknowledge that I am your Lord and Provider. This is the proper stance for a child of God: receiving with thanksgiving. Bring Me the sacrifice of gratitude, and watch to see how much I bless you.

"Rest in the deep assurance of My unfailing Love." What verses, promises, and experiences offer the deep assurance of God's unfailing Love for you personally?

....

....

....

....

....

Are there troubling things you need to release into His care? Do that now.

....

....

....

....

....

Write out your sacrifice of gratitude, and begin recording His blessings here.

....

....

....

....

....

READ MORE: 1 PETER 5:7; EPHESIANS 3:16–19

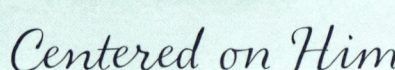

Centered on Him

Jesus replied: "'Love the Lord your God with all your
heart and with all your soul and with all your mind.'"

MATTHEW 22:37

COME TO ME CONTINUALLY. I am meant to be the Center of your consciousness, the *Anchor of your soul*. Your mind will wander from Me, but the question is how far you allow it to wander. An anchor on a short rope lets a boat drift only slightly before the taut line tugs the boat back toward the center. Similarly, as you drift away from Me, My Spirit within you gives a tug, prompting you to return to Me. As you become increasingly attuned to My Presence,

> *I am meant to be the Center of your consciousness, the Anchor of your soul.*

the length of rope on your soul's Anchor is shortened. You wander only a short distance before feeling that inner tug—telling you to return to your true Center in Me.

176

"Your mind will wander from Me, but the question is how far you allow it to wander." How far do you allow your mind to wander? Is it too far?

....

....

....

....

....

How should the command of Matthew 22:37 shape our thought-life?

....

....

....

....

....

Write out a prayer committing your thoughts to the Lord and asking Him to keep your mind centered on Him.

....

....

....

....

....

READ MORE: HEBREWS 6:19; 1 JOHN 2:28

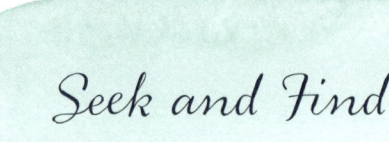

Seek and Find

When You said, "Seek My face," my heart
said to You, "Your face, LORD, I will seek."

PSALM 27:8 NKJV

SEEK MY FACE, and you will find more than you ever dreamed possible. *Let Me displace worry at the center of your being.* I am like a supersaturated cloud, showering Peace into the pool of your mind. My Nature is to bless. Your nature is to receive with thanksgiving. This is a true fit, designed before the foundation of the world. Glorify Me by receiving My blessings gratefully.

I am the goal of all your searching. *When you seek Me, you find Me* and are satisfied. When lesser goals capture your attention, I fade into the background of your life. I am still there, watching and waiting, but you function as if you were alone. Actually, My Light shines on every situation you will ever face. Live radiantly by expanding your focus to include Me in all your moments. Let nothing dampen your search for Me.

God promises, "When you seek Me, you find Me." How are you seeking Him?

....

....

....

....

....

Where do you find God?

....

....

....

....

....

In what ways can you ensure that you never stop seeking and finding God?

....

....

....

....

....

READ MORE: PHILIPPIANS 4:7 THE MESSAGE; JEREMIAH 29:13

A Sacrifice of Thanksgiving

Sacrifice thank offerings to God, fulfill
your vows to the Most High.

PSALM 50:14

THANK ME FOR THE GLORIOUS GIFT OF MY SPIRIT. This is like priming the pump of a well. As you bring Me the sacrifice of thanksgiving, regardless of your feelings, My Spirit is able to work more freely within you. This produces more thankfulness and more freedom, until you are overflowing with gratitude.

> *I shower blessings on you daily.*

I shower blessings on you daily, but sometimes you don't perceive them. When your mind is stuck on a negative focus, you see neither Me nor My gifts. In faith, thank Me for whatever is preoccupying your mind. This will clear the blockage so that you can find Me.

180

How can thanksgiving become a sacrifice to God?

....

....

....

....

....

"When your mind is stuck on a negative focus, you see neither Me nor My gifts." How do negative thoughts interfere with your perception of God's blessings?

....

....

....

....

....

How might praise work to "clear the blockage" between you and God?

....

....

....

....

....

READ MORE: 2 CORINTHIANS 5:5; 2 CORINTHIANS 3:17; PSALM 95:2 NKJV

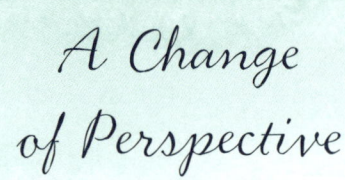

A Change of Perspective

Blessed are those who have learned to acclaim you,
who walk in the light of your presence, O LORD.

PSALM 89:15

WELCOME PROBLEMS as perspective-lifters. My children tend to sleepwalk through their days until they bump into an obstacle that stymies them.

If you encounter a problem with no immediate solution, your response to that situation will take you either up or down. You can lash out at the difficulty, resenting it and feeling sorry for yourself. This will take you down into a pit of self-pity. Alternatively, the problem can be a ladder, enabling you to climb up and see your life from My perspective. Viewed from above, the obstacle that frustrated you is only *a light and momentary trouble*. Once your perspective has been heightened, you can look away from the problem altogether. Turn toward Me, and see *the Light of My Presence* shining upon you.

When you encounter a problem with no easy or immediate solution, what is your typical response?

....

....

....

....

How would our view of problems change if we were to view them from God's perspective?

....

....

....

....

Read 2 Corinthians 4:16–18. How can problems encourage you to look beyond what is seen to what is unseen?

....

....

....

....

....

READ MORE: 2 CORINTHIANS 4:16–18

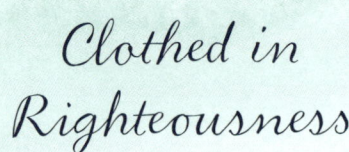

Clothed in Righteousness

I delight greatly in the LORD; my soul rejoices in my God. For
he has clothed me with garments of salvation and arrayed me
in a robe of righteousness, as a bridegroom adorns his head
like a priest, and as a bride adorns herself with her jewels.

ISAIAH 61:10

WHEN YOUR SINS WEIGH HEAVILY upon you, come to Me.
Confess your wrongdoing, which I know all about before you
say a word. Stay in the Light of My Presence, receiving forgiveness, cleansing, and healing. Remember that *I have clothed you
in My righteousness*, so nothing can separate you from Me.
Whenever you stumble or fall, I am there to help you up.

Man's tendency is to hide from his sin, seeking refuge
in the darkness. There he indulges in self-pity, denial, self-
righteousness, blaming, and hatred. But *I am the Light of the
world*, and My illumination decimates the darkness. Come close
to Me and let My Light envelop you, driving out darkness and
permeating you with Peace.

Are there sins weighing heavily on you? Are you ready for God to lift that burden? Lay them at His feet now.

....

....

....

....

Have you ever felt tempted to hide from your sins rather than laying them out in confession to God? Why?

....

....

....

....

"I have clothed you in My righteousness, so nothing can separate you from Me." What does this gift mean to you—today, tomorrow, and for eternity?

....

....

....

....

....

READ MORE: 1 JOHN 1:7; JOHN 8:12

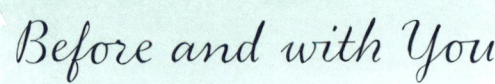

Before and with You

Therefore we do not lose heart. Though outwardly we are wasting away, yet inwardly we are being renewed day by day. For our light and momentary troubles are achieving for us an eternal glory that far outweighs them all.

2 CORINTHIANS 4:16–17

STAY CALMLY CONSCIOUS OF ME today, no matter what. Remember that I go before you as well as with you into the day. Nothing takes Me by surprise. I will not allow circumstances to overwhelm you so long as you look to Me. I will help you cope with whatever the moment presents. Collaborating with Me brings *blessings that far outweigh all your troubles.* Awareness of My Presence contains Joy that can endure all eventualities.

> *Remember that I go before you as well as with you into the day.*

"How does your awareness of the omnipresence of God help you to trust Him more?

....

....

....

....

Nothing takes God by surprise. What assurance does that give you for the unknowns of your day?

....

....

....

....

How does collaborating with God bring "blessings that far outweigh all your troubles"? How have you seen this happen in your own life?

....

....

....

....

....

READ MORE: PSALM 23:1–4 NKJV; PSALM 28:7

Your Loved Ones

The LORD replied, "My Presence will go
with you, and I will give you rest."

EXODUS 33:14

ENTRUST YOUR LOVED ONES TO ME; release them into My protective care. They are much safer with Me than in your clinging hands. If you let a loved one become an idol in your heart, you endanger that one—as well as yourself. Joseph and his father, Jacob, suffered terribly because Jacob *loved Joseph more than any of his other sons* and treated him with special favor. So Joseph's brothers hated him and plotted against him. Ultimately, I used that situation for good, but both father and son had to endure years of suffering and separation from one another.

I detest idolatry, even in the form of parental love, so beware of making a beloved child your idol. When you release loved ones to Me, you are free to cling to My hand. As you entrust others into My care, I am free to shower blessings on them. *My Presence will go with them wherever they go, and I will give them rest*. This same Presence stays with you as you relax and place your trust in Me. Watch to see what I will do.

Why are your loved ones safer in God's hands than in "your clinging hands"? Is there someone you need to entrust to God's care?

....

....

....

....

Why is it dangerous to let a loved one become an idol in our hearts?

....

....

....

....

Write out a prayer entrusting your loved ones to God's care and keeping.

....

....

....

....

READ MORE: EPHESIANS 3:20; GENESIS 37:3–4

In All Circumstances

Enter his gates with thanksgiving and his courts with
praise; give thanks to him and praise his name.

PSALM 100:4

THANKFULNESS OPENS THE DOOR to My Presence. Though I am always with you, I have gone to great measures to preserve your freedom of choice. I have placed a door between you and Me, and I have empowered you to open or close that door. There are many ways to open it, but a grateful attitude is one of the most effective.

Thankfulness is built on a substructure of trust. When thankful words stick in your throat, you need to check up on your foundation of trust. When thankfulness flows freely from your heart and lips, let your gratitude draw you closer to Me. I want you to learn the art of *giving thanks in all circumstances*. See how many times you can thank Me daily; this will awaken your awareness to a multitude of blessings. It will also cushion the impact of trials when they come against you. Practice My Presence by practicing the discipline of thankfulness.

"Thankfulness opens the door to My Presence." In what ways have you seen this truth in your life?

....

....

....

....

What is the relationship between thankfulness and trust? If our trust is faltering, what needs to happen with thankfulness?

....

....

....

....

Are you able to give thanks in any circumstance? How many times can you thank God today?

....

....

....

....

....

READ MORE: PSALM 31:14; THESSALONIANS 5:18

Staying in the Present

Let us hold unswervingly to the hope we
profess, for he who promised is faithful.

HEBREWS 10:23

TRUST ME AND REFUSE TO WORRY, for *I am your Strength and Song.* You are feeling wobbly this morning, looking at difficult times looming ahead, measuring them against your own strength. However, they are not today's tasks—or even tomorrow's. So leave them in the future and come home to the present, where you will find Me waiting for you. Since *I am your Strength,* I can empower you to handle each task as it comes. Because *I am your Song,* I can give you Joy as you work alongside Me.

Keep bringing your mind back to the present moment. Among all My creatures, only humans can anticipate future events. This ability is a blessing, but it becomes a curse whenever it is misused. If you use your magnificent mind to worry about tomorrow, you cloak yourself in dark unbelief. However, when the hope of heaven fills your thoughts, the Light of My

Presence envelops you. Though heaven is future, it is also present tense. As you walk in the Light with Me, you have one foot on earth and one foot in heaven.

Are you often tempted to pick up tomorrow's tasks today?

....

....

....

....

When our thoughts wander to the future, what practical things can we do to bring our minds back to the present?

....

....

....

....

How is heaven both future and present tense? What hope does this give you?

....

....

....

....

READ MORE: EXODUS 15:2; 2 CORINTHIANS 10:5

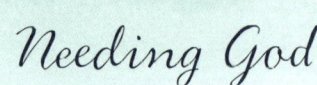

Needing God

The eternal God is your refuge, and underneath
are the everlasting arms. He will drive out your
enemy before you, saying, "Destroy him!"

DEUTERONOMY 33:27

RELAX IN *MY EVERLASTING ARMS.* Your weakness is an opportunity to grow strong in awareness of My Almighty Presence. When your energy fails you, do not look inward and lament the lack you find there. Look to Me and My sufficiency; rejoice in My radiant riches that are abundantly available to help you.

> *Go gently through this day, leaning on Me and enjoying My Presence.*

Go gently through this day, leaning on Me and enjoying My Presence. Thank Me for your neediness, which is building trust-bonds between us. If you look back on your journey thus far, you can see that days of extreme weakness have been some of your most precious times. Memories of these days are richly interwoven with golden strands of My intimate Presence.

"Relax in My everlasting arms." What would this look like in your life today?

....

....

....

....

How does our neediness help to build our trust in God? How have you found Him to be reliable—even if in unexpected ways?

....

....

....

....

When you look back on your journey, when do you see that God carried you?

....

....

....

....

READ MORE: DEUTERONOMY 33:27; ROMANS 8:26; PSALM 27:13–14

The Unfairness of Life

Bear with each other and forgive whatever grievances you may
have against one another. Forgive as the Lord forgave you.

COLOSSIANS 3:13

DO NOT EXPECT to be treated fairly in this life. People will say and
do hurtful things to you, things that you don't deserve. When
someone mistreats you, try to view it as an opportunity to grow in
grace. See how quickly you can forgive the one who has wounded
you. Don't be concerned about setting the record straight. Instead
of obsessing about other people's opinions of you, keep your focus
on Me. Ultimately, it is My view of you that counts.

As you concentrate on relating to Me, remember that I have
clothed you in My righteousness and holiness. I see you attired
in these radiant garments, which I bought for you with My
blood. This also is not fair; it is pure gift. When others treat
you unfairly, remember that My ways with you are much better
than fair. My ways are Peace and *Love, which I have poured out
into your heart by My Spirit.*

Do you ever find yourself surprised by the unfairness of life? When have you felt this way?

....

....

....

....

How can being unfairly treated be transformed into an opportunity to grow in grace? Do you have that opportunity in your life now?

....

....

....

....

....

How have you been blessed by an unfair situation and God's gifts to you?

....

....

....

....

....

READ MORE: ISAIAH 61:10; EPHESIANS 1:7–8; ROMANS 5:5

Focusing on God

Then will I go to the altar of God, to God,
my joy and my delight. I will praise you
with the harp, O God, my God.

PSALM 43:4

SPEND TIME WITH ME for the pure pleasure of being in My company. I can brighten up the dullest of gray days; I can add sparkle to the routines of daily life. You have to repeat so many tasks day after day. This monotony can dull your thinking until your mind slips into neutral. A mind that is unfocused is vulnerable to the world, the flesh, and the devil, all of which exert a downward pull on your thoughts. As

> I can brighten up the dullest of gray days.

your thinking processes deteriorate, you become increasingly confused and directionless. The best remedy is to refocus your mind and heart on Me, your constant Companion.

Even the most confusing day opens up before you as you go

step by step with Me. My Presence goes with you wherever you go, providing *Light for your path.*

How can spending time with God and seeking out His Presence in each moment add sparkle to your life?

....

....

....

....

An unfocused mind is "vulnerable to the world, the flesh, and the devil." Have you seen this truth in your life or in the lives of others?

....

....

....

....

What are some practical ways you can "refocus your mind and heart" on God?

....

....

....

....

READ MORE: PSALM 63:7–8; PSALM 119:105

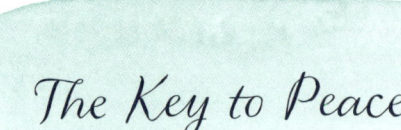

The Key to Peace

"Peace I leave with you, My peace I give to you;
not as the world gives do I give to you. Let not
your heart be troubled, neither let it be afraid."

JOHN 14:27 NKJV

LET ME INFUSE MY PEACE into your innermost being. As you sit quietly in the Light of My Presence, you can sense Peace growing within you. This is not something that you accomplish through self-discipline and willpower; it is opening yourself to receive My blessing.

In this age of independence, people find it hard to acknowledge their neediness. However, I have taken you along a path that has highlighted your need for Me, placing you in situations where your strengths were irrelevant and your weaknesses were glaringly evident. Through the aridity of those desert marches, I have drawn you closer and closer to Myself. You have discovered flowers of Peace blossoming in the most desolate places. You have learned to thank Me for hard times and difficult journeys, trusting that through them I accomplish My best work. You have realized that needing Me is the key to knowing Me intimately, which is the gift above all gifts.

The Peace of God is not something we can attain by "self-discipline and willpower." What is the secret to filling your life with His Peace?

....

....

....

....

Do you struggle to admit your need for God? Why?

....

....

....

....

Needing God is crucial to knowing Him. How have you seen this truth in your life?

....

....

....

READ MORE: ISAIAH 58:11; ISAIAH 40:11

Learning to Listen

"Do not come any closer," God said. "Take
off your sandals, for the place where
you are standing is holy ground."

EXODUS 3:5

LEARN TO LISTEN TO ME even while you are listening to other people. As they open their souls to your scrutiny, *you are on holy ground.* You need the help of My Spirit to respond appropriately. Ask Him to think through you, live through you, love through you. My own Being is alive within you in the Person of the Holy Spirit. If you respond to others' needs through your unaided thought processes, you offer them dry crumbs. When the Spirit empowers your listening and speaking, My *streams of living water flow* through you to other people. Be a channel of My Love, Joy, and Peace by listening to Me as you listen to others.

Why is obeying God, even when you're listening to others, important to practice?

....

....

....

....

When others come to you for advice, guidance, comfort, or simply a listening ear, what responsibility do you have toward them? How is this "holy ground"?

....

....

....

....

Write out a prayer asking God "to think through you, live through you, love through you."

....

....

....

....

....

READ MORE: 1 CORINTHIANS 6:19; JOHN 7:38–39

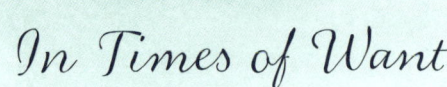

In Times of Want

And He has said to me, "My grace is sufficient for
you, for power is perfected in weakness." Most gladly,
therefore, I will rather boast about my weaknesses,
so that the power of Christ may dwell in me.

2 CORINTHIANS 12:9 NASB

WHEN SOME BASIC NEED IS LACKING—time, energy, money—consider yourself blessed. Your very lack is an opportunity to latch onto Me in unashamed dependence. When you begin a day with inadequate resources, you must concentrate your efforts on the present moment. This is where you are meant to live—in the present. It is the place where I always await you. Awareness of your inadequacy is a rich blessing, training you to rely wholeheartedly on Me.

> *Rejoice in your insufficiency, knowing that My Power is made perfect in weakness.*

The truth is that self-sufficiency is a myth perpetuated by pride and temporary success. Health and wealth can disappear instantly, as can life itself. Rejoice in your insufficiency, knowing that *My Power is made perfect in weakness.*

How is self-sufficiency perpetuated by pride and temporary successes?

....

....

....

....

How can the lack of a basic need cause you to draw closer to God? Have you experienced this yourself?

....

....

....

Do you find yourself able to "rejoice in your insufficiency"? How does your weakness make room for the power of God?

....

....

....

READ MORE: JAMES 1:2–3

In Uncertainty

"I am the Alpha and the Omega, the First
and the Last, the Beginning and the End."

REVELATION 22:13

IN A WORLD OF UNRELENTING CHANGES, I am the One who
never changes. *I am the Alpha and the Omega, the First and the
Last, the Beginning and the End.* Find in Me the stability for
which you have yearned.

I created a beautifully ordered world: one that reflects My
perfection. Now, however, the world is under the bondage of
sin and evil. Every person on the planet faces gaping jaws of
uncertainty. The only antidote to this poisonous threat is draw-
ing closer to Me. In My Presence you can face uncertainty with
perfect Peace.

What are the uncertainties that plague you?

....

....

....

....

Does the unchanging nature of God give you confidence to face an ever-changing world?

....

....

....

....

....

How has the reality of God's Presence allowed you to experience His Peace in uncertain times?

....

....

....

....

....

READ MORE: ROMANS 5:12; JOHN 16:33 AMP

In the Morning

In the morning, O LORD, you hear my
voice; in the morning I lay my requests
before you and wait in expectation.

PSALM 5:3

AS YOU GET OUT OF BED in the morning, be aware of My Presence with you. You may not be thinking clearly yet, but I am. Your early morning thoughts tend to be anxious ones until you get connected with Me. Invite Me into your thoughts by whispering My Name. Suddenly your day brightens and feels more user-friendly. You cannot dread a day that is vibrant with My Presence.

You gain confidence through knowing that I am with you— that you face nothing alone. Anxiety stems from asking the wrong question: "If such and such happens, can I handle it?" The true question is not whether you can cope with whatever happens, but whether you and I together can handle anything that occurs. It is this you-and-I-together factor that gives you confidence to face the day cheerfully.

Where do your thoughts usually go first thing in the morning? What can you do to direct them to God?

....

....

....

....

"Anxiety stems from asking the wrong question: 'If such and such happens, can I handle it?'" Why is this the wrong question to ask? What should we ask instead?

....

....

....

....

Write out a prayer inviting God into your thoughts and your day.

....

....

....

....

....

READ MORE: PSALM 63:1 NKJV; PHILIPPIANS 4:13

A God Who Gives

You will keep him in perfect peace, whose mind
is stayed on You, because he trusts in You.

ISAIAH 26:3 NKJV

I AM A GOD WHO GIVES and gives and gives. When I died for you on the cross, I held back nothing; I poured out My Life *like a drink offering.* Because giving is inherent in My nature, I search for people who are able to receive in full measure. To increase your intimacy with Me, the two traits you need the most are receptivity and attentiveness. Receptivity is opening up your innermost being to be filled with My abundant riches. Attentiveness is directing your gaze to Me, searching for Me in all your moments. It is possible to *stay your mind on Me,* as the prophet Isaiah wrote. Through such attentiveness you receive a glorious gift: My perfect Peace.

What has God given you?

....

....

....

....

....

Is receiving from God something that comes easily to you? What hinders you?

....

....

....

....

....

How might continually searching for God fill all your moments with His Peace?

....

....

....

....

....

READ MORE: PHILIPPIANS 2:17; MARK 10:15

His Constant and Encouraging Presence

"And teaching them to obey everything I
have commanded you. And surely I am with
you always, to the very end of the age."

TRUST ME IN THE DEPTHS of your being. It is there that I live in constant communion with you. When you feel flustered and frazzled on the outside, do not get upset with yourself. You are only human, and the swirl of events going on all around you will sometimes feel overwhelming. Rather than scolding yourself for your humanness, remind yourself that I am both with you and within you.

I am with you at all times, encouraging and supportive rather than condemning. I know that deep within you, where I live, My Peace is your continual experience. Slow down your pace of living for a time. Quiet your mind in My Presence. Then you will be able to hear Me bestowing the resurrection blessing: *Peace be with you.*

When are you most overwhelmed? Do you get upset with yourself for being overwhelmed? How can you respond differently?

....

....

....

....

What can we do to remind ourselves of God's constant and encouraging Presence?

....

....

....

....

What does Christ's resurrection blessing—"Peace be with you"—offer you? How does it make you feel to know God gives you His Peace every day?

....

....

....

....

....

READ MORE: COLOSSIANS 1:27; JOHN 20:19

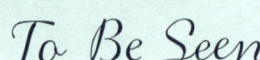

To Be Seen

Where can I go from your Spirit? Where can I flee
from your presence? If I go up to the heavens, you
are there; if I make my bed in the depths, you are
there. If I rise on the wings of the dawn, if I settle
on the far side of the sea, even there your hand
will guide me, your right hand will hold me fast.

PSALM 139:7–10

THERE IS NO PLACE so desolate that you cannot find Me there. When Hagar fled from her mistress, Sarah, into the wilderness, she thought she was utterly alone and forsaken. But Hagar encountered Me in that desolate place. There she addressed Me as *the Living One who sees me*. Through that encounter with My Presence, she gained courage to return to her mistress.

No set of circumstances could ever isolate you from My loving Presence. Not only do I see you always, I see you as a redeemed saint, gloriously radiant in My righteousness. That is why *I take great delight in you and rejoice over you with singing!*

Have you ever felt that God couldn't find you? Read Psalm 139:7–10. What is the truth about being found by God?

....

....

....

....

Hagar called God "the Living One who sees me." What does it mean to you to be truly seen by God?

....

....

....

....

Do you see yourself as "a redeemed saint, gloriously radiant" in God's righteousness? What changes can you make to start seeing yourself through God's eyes?

....

....

....

....

READ MORE: GENESIS 16:13–14 AMP; ZEPHANIAH 3:17

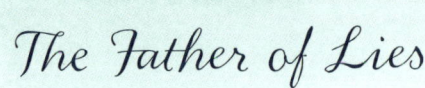

The Father of Lies

"You belong to your father, the devil, and you want to carry out your father's desire. . . . When he lies, he speaks his native language, for he is a liar and the father of lies."

JOHN 8:44

OPEN YOUR MIND AND HEART—your entire being—to receive My Love in full measure. So many of My children limp through their lives starved for Love because they haven't learned the art of receiving. This is essentially an act of faith: believing that I love you with boundless, everlasting Love. The art of receiving is also a discipline: training your mind to trust Me, coming close to Me with confidence.

Remember that the evil one is *the father of lies*. Learn to recognize his deceptive intrusions into your thoughts. One of his favorite deceptions is to undermine your confidence in My unconditional Love. Fight back against these lies! Do not let them go unchallenged. *Resist the devil in My Name, and he will slink away from you. Draw near to Me*, and My Presence will envelop you in Love.

Have you opened your mind and heart to receive God's Love in full measure? Is something holding you back? What is it?

....
....
....
....

What lies is the father of lies whispering to you? Write out a verse proclaiming God's truth for each of those lies.

....
....
....
....

One of the devil's favorite deceptions is to undermine our confidence in God's love. What is the truth about God's unconditional love for you?

....
....
....
....
....

READ MORE: EPHESIANS 3:16–18; HEBREWS 4:16; JAMES 4:7–8 NKJV

The Truly Important

I will instruct you and teach you in the way you
should go; I will counsel you and watch over you.

PSALM 32:8

PROBLEMS ARE PART OF LIFE. They are inescapable, woven into the very fabric of this fallen world. You tend to go into problem-solving mode all too readily, acting as if you have the capacity to fix everything. This is a habitual response, so automatic that it bypasses your conscious thinking. Not only does this habit frustrate you, it also distances you from Me.

Do not let fixing things be your top priority. You are ever so limited in your capacity to correct all that is wrong in the world around you. Don't weigh yourself down with responsibilities that are not your own. Instead, make your relationship with Me your primary concern. Talk with Me about whatever is on your mind, seeking My perspective on the situation. Rather than trying to fix everything that comes to your attention, ask Me to show you what is truly important. Remember that you are *en route* to heaven, and let your problems fade in the Light of eternity.

Do you often default to problem-solving mode when troubles come your way? How can you change your response to problems?

....

....

....

....

What should be your top priority?

....

....

....

....

....

Read Luke 10:41–42. Are you choosing what is "truly important"? Write out a prayer asking God to show you what is most important to Him.

....

....

....

....

....

READ MORE: LUKE 10:41–42; PHILIPPIANS 3:20–21

The Gift of God

But I trust in your unfailing love; my
heart rejoices in your salvation.

PSALM 13:5

I AM THE GIFT that continuously gives—bounteously, with no strings attached. Unconditional Love is such a radical concept that even My most devoted followers fail to grasp it fully. Absolutely nothing in heaven or on earth can cause Me to stop loving you. You may *feel* more loved when you are performing according to your expectations. But My Love for you is perfect; therefore it is not subject to variation. What *does* vary is your awareness of My loving Presence.

I am the gift that continuously gives.

When you are dissatisfied with your behavior, you tend to feel unworthy of My Love. You may unconsciously punish yourself by withdrawing from Me and attributing the distance between us to My displeasure. Instead of returning to Me and receiving My

Love, you attempt to earn My approval by trying harder. All the while, I am aching to hold you in *My everlasting arms*, to enfold you in My Love. When you are feeling unworthy or unloved, come to Me. Then ask for receptivity to *My unfailing Love.*

We often talk about the gifts God pours into our lives. How is God the greatest gift of all?

....

....

....

....

....

When you have not lived up to your expectations or God's, are you tempted to pull away and hide from Him? What does He want you to do instead?

....

....

....

....

....

....

Read More: 1 John 4:15–16, 18; Deuteronomy 33:27

His Leading

"Remain in me, and I will remain in you. No branch
can bear fruit by itself; it must remain in the vine.
Neither can you bear fruit unless you remain in me."

JOHN 15:4

I AM LEADING YOU along a way that is uniquely right for you.
The closer to Me you grow, the more fully you become your
true self—the one I designed you to be. Because you are one of
a kind, the path you are traveling with Me diverges increasingly
from that of other people. However, in My mysterious wisdom
and ways, I enable you to follow this solitary path while staying
in close contact with others. In fact, the more completely you
devote yourself to Me, the more freely you can love people.

Marvel at the beauty of a life intertwined with My Presence.
Rejoice as we journey together in intimate communion. Enjoy
the adventure of finding yourself through losing yourself in Me.

The path God has for you is intensely personal. What does this tell you about God and His leading in your life?

....

....

....

....

....

Who do you see God leading you to become?

....

....

....

....

....

How has your closeness to God enabled you to better love those around you?

....

....

....

....

....

READ MORE: 2 CORINTHIANS 5:17; EPHESIANS 2:10; 1 JOHN 4:7–8

Source Guide

All entries taken from *Jesus Calling*

Hope. . . . . July 27
The Goodness of God. . . . . .June 28
Thankfulness . . . . .January 17
Following Him. . . . . March 3
His Presence . . . . .October 25
Rest . . . . .February 6
You Are Known . . . . September 16
Abundance. . . . . .March 23
Anxiety and Fear . . . . July 19
Every Moment . . . . February 22
Time with Him . . . . January 2
Follow Me . . . . .February 1
Constant Communication. . . . . April 1
Cease Striving . . . . June 2
Distractions and Worries . . . . .September 3
God Is Near. . . . . October 2
Hide in Him . . . . January 3
Complete . . . . April 3
Refuse to Worry . . . . March 4
The Beauty of Holiness. . . . . .May 4
Chasing Perfection . . . . June 5
Judgment . . . . July 3
When Everything Goes Wrong . . . . August 6
His Path. . . . . .May 1
Expectations . . . . November 4
Soak in His Presence . . . . July 1
Protected . . . . December 1
In Weakness . . . . .February 4
Potter and Clay . . . . April 7
Finding Him . . . . .February 2
The Important and Unimportant. . . . . . . .May 6
Depending on Jesus. . . . . January 5
Transformed. . . . . June 8
Thanksgiving and Trust . . . . July 7
Healing . . . . August 10
Always Available . . . . September 10
True Joy. . . . . October 5
Close to Him . . . . November 5
With You and for You. . . . . January 9
Goals and God's Will. . . . . March 8
Your Strength and Song . . . . .June 11
Come to Him. . . . . August 11
Without Complaint. . . . . October 9
Difficult Days . . . . November 8
Complete in Him . . . . December 8
Slowing Down . . . . February 10
You Are His . . . . .March 10
Moment by Moment . . . . April 12
Mistakes . . . . .May 9
Unseen Things. . . . . .June 15
The Pit of Self-Pity . . . . July 16
Equipped for Trouble . . . . .May 8
God with You . . . . August 13
Unconditional Love. . . . . September 15
Through His Eyes . . . . .October 12

Understood and Loved . . . . November 14
Filling the Emptiness . . . . December 17
Saturated in Grace. . . . . .January 14
The Adventure of Today . . . . February 14
Wait, Trust, Hope . . . . .March 12
Loving Others . . . . May 12
Your Path. . . . . .June 16
What Is Better . . . . July 17
Present and Future . . . . April 14
Nothing to Fear . . . . August 14
Pleasing Him. . . . . November 20
Clearing the Clutter. . . . . December 19
Battling Addiction and Temptation . . . . January 15
Receiving Joy. . . . . .March 14
A Continual Gift of Peace . . . . April 18
Making Plans . . . . May 16
God Speaks. . . . . .June 20
In the Maelstrom . . . . August 17
Treasures in His Presence . . . . November 23
Patience and Trust . . . . December 21
Weighed Down . . . . February 19
A Cheerful Heart . . . . .March 16
His Love . . . . April 19
Safe and Secure . . . . May 19
Time for God. . . . . .June 21
Thirsting for God . . . . July 20
In Adversity . . . . August 18
The Freedom of Forgiveness. . . . . . . September 23
Joy in His Presence . . . . .October 22
Deep Assurance . . . . November 28
Centered on Him . . . . July 29
Seek and Find . . . . .January 19
A Sacrifice of Thanksgiving . . . . March 20
A Change of Perspective . . . . April 26
Clothed in Righteousness . . . . May 20
Before and with You. . . . . .June 26
Your Loved Ones . . . . August 23
In All Circumstances. . . . . July 24
Staying in the Present. . . . . September 22
Needing God. . . . . September 27
The Unfairness of Life . . . . .October 28
Focusing on God . . . . August 27
The Key to Peace. . . . . November 29
Learning to Listen. . . . . .October 31
In Times of Want . . . . April 30
In Uncertainty. . . . . May 26
In the Morning . . . . .June 29
A God Who Gives. . . . . March 28
His Constant and Encouraging Presence . . . July 31
To Be Seen . . . . August 30
The Father of Lies . . . . September 28
The Truly Important . . . . November 30
The Gift of God . . . . December 26
His Leading . . . . December 30